Pawns of War

DWIGHT R. MESSIMER

Pawns of War

THE LOSS OF THE USS *LANGLEY* AND THE USS *PECOS*

NAVAL INSTITUTE PRESS   ANNAPOLIS, MARYLAND

Copyright © 1983
by the United States Naval Institute
Annapolis, Maryland

Library of Congress Cataloging in Publication Data
Messimer, Dwight R., 1937-
    Pawns of war.
    Bibliography: p.
    Includes index.
    1. Langley (Aircraft carrier) 2. Pecos (Ship)
3. World War, 1939–1945—Pacific Ocean. 4. World War, 1939–1945—Naval
operations, American. I. Title.
D774.L32M47   1982   940.54'5973   82-14415
ISBN 0-87021-515-9

Printed in the United States of America

To my son
Dale

Contents

Preface

In 1943 my older brother showed me a long, wooden cheese box, across the top of which he had nailed a thin piece of wood. It looked to me like a box with an oversized lid. He said it was an aircraft carrier. Many years later I was looking through a book and saw a photograph of a ship that looked remarkably similar to my brother's cheese box flat-top. The caption identified the ship as the USS *Langley* (CV-1), and said that she was America's first aircraft carrier.

I ran across the *Langley* again while researching *No Margin for Error* and became interested in her. The 1920s and early 1930s were her golden years, and her contributions to naval aviation during those years are frequently written about. But the details of her career end abruptly in 1936, and historically she all but vanishes. The accounts usually end with a simple statement that she was sunk in the early days of World War II.

To find out what happened to the *Langley*, I read hundreds of documents and interviewed over one hundred survivors or participants in her mission. What I learned was both exciting and infuriating. This is the story of a proud, old ship sent on a pointless mission to serve a hopeless cause. Political expediency, bureaucratic bumbling, and indecision cost the Navy three ships and nearly 800 men.

The purpose of this book is to provide, for the first time, the details of the *Langley*'s loss. It is also intended to give recognition to the officers and men of the *Langley* and the USS *Pecos* (A0-6).

The task of acknowledging all the people who generously contributed material and assisted in the writing of this book is one that must be approached with care. There are simply too many for all to be named individually here. Collectively, all the *Langley* and *Pecos* survivors are the people to whom I am most indebted, followed closely by the former *Langley* (CV-1) crewmen and the Air Force men who answered my call for help. Those men are all named in the bibliography, and most appear in the text. There were those who had more to say, who loaned me their private papers, or who provided extraordinarily valuable photographs. But each contribution, whether large or small, was vital. It would, therefore, be unfair to select only a few for special recognition. My thanks goes out to them all.

There are, however, people whose names do not appear anywhere in this book, who nevertheless made substantial contributions and deserve recognition. Joanne MacDougal, a lady who remains pleasant in the most trying circumstances, was my frequently used back-up typist. She got me out of more than one tight spot as the deadline closed in. My good friend George Moore translated the Japanese documents even when he had his own commitments—an act of friendship that is going to be hard to repay. My mother did her usual thorough job of proofreading, and kept me from looking like a moron in the eyes of the editor. Kirk Autsen accepted every change I made in the drawings without complaint, even though the changes were nearly always made on the "final" drawing.

Special thanks go to Dean Allard and his staff at the Naval Historical Center for the great service they performed by providing me with most of the documents used in this book.

Lastly, I must thank my wife who typed and retyped the manuscript, handled my correspondence, fixed meals, and kept house without once threatening divorce.

Pawns of War

CHAPTER 1

The *Langley*

The Japanese pilot spotted three ships zig-zagging across the smooth surface of the sea. He banked his twin-engine bomber, dropping the left wing for a better view. Below him were—his pulse rate jumped—a cruiser, a destroyer, and—he leaned closer to the plexiglas—an aircraft carrier! His radioman pounded out the message: ENEMY CARRIER X MANY PLANES X ESCORT-CRUISER-DESTROYER X POSITION X COURSE X SPEED X . . . the bomber rolled over on the other wing and roared away.[1]

The sighting report was received by the Takao Air Group headquarters on Bali, just 360 miles away. While aircrews were being briefed, their planes were bombed-up and fuel tanks were topped-off. Within fifty minutes sixteen twin-engine, Mitsubishi, G3M2 (Nell) bombers were airborne. Eight minutes later they were joined by fifteen Zero fighters.

As the bombers and fighters streaked across the southeast tip of Java, the lead bombardier/navigator worked out the course for interception and figured the time to target. He wrote his estimate on a piece of paper and thrust it up to the pilot who sat above and behind him. The pilot took the note and read, "Course 265 degrees, true: time to target, 2 hours." The lead bombardier/navigator was right on the money.

Excellence was a standard that the Japanese Navy had come to expect of its aircrews, and the men in the thirty-one fighters and bombers met that standard. Every one was a veteran of the war in China and the Philippines. A squadron leader in the fighter escort, Lieutenant Tamotsu Yokoyama, was rated by the Japanese as one of Japan's ten best "fighter-plane strategists and pilots."[2] As the planes raced toward the target, the bomber crews thought that this was their opportunity to accomplish part of what had not been done at Pearl Harbor—the destruction of America's aircraft carriers. In the Zeros' cockpits the fighter pilots eagerly anticipated a chance to test the skill of American naval aviators.

Disappointingly for those men, the Japanese Navy's standard of excellence had not been fully met by the reconnaissance pilot. He had incorrectly identified two of the three ships. What he thought was a cruiser was really an old "four-piper" destroyer. But from a distance, and through a haze of excitement, a four-piper may have looked like a cruiser. Why the other, identical destroyer looked less like a cruiser is not clear.

He was also wrong about the carrier. What he had really seen was the seaplane tender, USS Langley *(AV-3). The old ship had once been an aircraft carrier; in fact, she had been CV-1, the U.S. Navy's first aircraft carrier. On her flight deck naval aviation in its most lethal form had been born, nurtured, and developed. The Japanese pilots were in for a disappointment, but their target was, nonetheless, more than just another ship. The* Langley *was a piece of American history.*

In the summer of 1939, the USS *Langley* (AV-3) lay anchored in San Diego Harbor, preparing to depart for her new assignment with the Asiatic Fleet. The threat of war in Europe grew larger each day, and in the Pacific Japan was becoming increasingly hostile toward the Western powers. On the *Langley's* signal bridge, Seaman First Class Paul St. Pierre was discussing with a friend the possibility of war. The seaplane tender's upcoming assignment to Asian duty gave the subject added importance, and St. Pierre raised the question of how the *Langley* would fare in battle.[3]

His friend did not answer immediately, his attention apparently fixed on a speedboat that raced across the harbor and started to circle the ship. When he did answer, he spoke with the conviction of a man who strongly believed what he said.

"If we get into a war, the *Langley* better be up the Mississippi."

"What does that mean?" St. Pierre demanded. "She's as good as any other ship and can take care of herself in any battle."

"Let me tell you somethin', ole buddy. This ole bucket's only got hull plates an inch thick, and she won't do more'n 14 knots.

She's so old she rattles and squeaks, and if she gets into a shooting war, she won't have a Chinaman's chance in hell."

The speedboat completed its circle around the tender, and the sailor paused to wave to the grinning occupants. Before St. Pierre could protest, the man continued.

"See that speedboat down there? All the Japs gotta do is drop one of them in the water with a machine gun in the bow, and then run circles around us while they cut the bottom off."

St. Pierre remained unconvinced, insisting that the ship "would do better than that." Two and a half years later, after being discharged following a serious injury, Paul St. Pierre was reminded of the conversation. In March 1942 while he was reading the bleak war news, he saw a column headlined, "AIRCRAFT TENDER, OTHER VESSELS SUNK IN THE LAST TWO MONTHS."[4] Among the ships named were the *Langley* and the fleet oiler USS *Pecos* (AO-6). Additional information was sparse, but the loss of life was put at nearly 700 men. St. Pierre did not know how many of his old shipmates had been in the *Langley* when she went down, but in March 1942 he wished she had been up the Mississippi instead of in the Indian Ocean.

St. Pierre's friend may have overstated his case, but he was absolutely right about the *Langley* being old and vulnerable. She had been built before World War I as a coal collier, and though later converted to an aircraft carrier, she was never intended to fill a warship's role. During her entire career she was either an auxiliary or an experimental platform.

The Mare Island Navy Yard launched her in 1912 as the coal collier USS *Jupiter* (AC-3). Even then she was something of a test bed, being the first U.S. Navy ship to be equipped with a turbine-electric propulsion system. Known as the Melville-McAlpine Electric Drive, the propulsion system was composed of two huge electric motors that in turn were powered by steam-turbine engines. The system, if not the brand, was later adopted for use in the *California*- and *Maryland*-class battleships.[5]

The *Jupiter* established at least two more notable "firsts" before she was converted. In 1914 she became the first ship to transit the Panama Canal from west to east, and in 1917 she carried part of the First Aeronautic Detachment of the U.S. Navy from Hoboken

The *Jupiter* at Mare Island in October 1913. When this picture was taken, no one could have guessed that this ungainly ship would become the progenitor of U.S. Navy carrier aviation. (National Archives)

to St. Nazaire. Not only was the First Aeronautic Detachment the first American combat unit to reach France after the declaration of war, but the *Jupiter* also delivered her contingent ahead of the section carried by the USS *Neptune* (AC-1).[6] In this instance, the *Jupiter* was the first of the first, and this transportation of the naval aviation unit was an unrecognized hint at what the future held for her.

By 1919 the wheels of progress were rolling slowly toward a proposal to provide the Navy with an aircraft carrier. But because it was such a revolutionary proposal in naval warfare, it was resisted by those who felt threatened by it. To determine the feasibility of their claims, the carrier advocates, overcoming heavy opposition, cleared the way for the construction of an aircraft carrier. But rather than build a carrier—a process both prohibitively expensive and time consuming—it was decided to convert an existing hull. Several ships were considered for conversion, and from them the *Jupiter* was selected.[7]

Despite the objections of such formidable opponents as the Chief of Naval Operations, Admiral William S. Benson, the *Jupiter* was decommissioned on 24 March 1920 and entered the Norfolk Navy Yard for conversion. Her original electric drive was replaced with a General Electric model; towers, booms, and winches were removed; gasoline storage tanks were installed beneath the bridge structure; and a layer of concrete ballast ten feet deep was poured over the keel. Coal bunkers became work shops, storerooms, and quarters. A wooden flight deck 534 feet long and 65 feet wide covered the entire hull.

Almost two years later to the day, on 20 March 1922, the USS *Langley* (CV-1) hoisted her commissioning pennant.[8] Homely, slow, and a little clumsy, she soon became known as the "covered wagon"—partly because of her ungainly appearance. She was, however, America's first entry in the race for air superiority at sea. In 1922 the United States Navy was far behind the leader, the Royal Navy, and the *Langley*'s arrival on the scene hardly made it appear that the Americans would soon catch up with, and pass, the leader.

The man most responsible for seeing that the *Langley* experiment worked was her executive officer, Commander Kenneth Whiting. Seven months after she was commissioned, Whiting was ready to take the first step toward making carrier aviation in the U.S. Navy a reality. The time had come to launch the first plane from the *Langley*'s flight deck.

The feat was not as simple as it sounds. A 500-foot run might be long enough to get a Vought VE-7-SF into the air. On the other hand it might not be. Whiting was not taking any chances, and he was also thinking ahead to future operating conditions. The requirement, therefore, was to get the plane into the air with the shortest possible run. The apparent solution would be to run the engine up to full power, release the brakes, and take off. The problem with that easy answer is that in 1922 planes did not have brakes, and wheel chocks would not hold a VE-7-SF at full power. The two-part solution was provided by Lieutenant Fred W. Pennoyer.[9]

When the big day arrived, Lieutenant Virgil C. Griffin walked across the flight deck toward the lone, single-seat fighter. The nettings along both edges of the flight deck were filled with people, and more excited spectators were lined up on the nearby shores of the York River. It was a cold, clear day. The *Langley* had been hauled into the wind with the aid of special buoyed anchors, allowing the October wind to blow straight down the flight deck.

Mechanics and deck crewmen were completing their final checks on the biplane as Griffin climbed into the tiny cockpit. The plane's tail skid rested in a shallow trough placed across two sawhorses, so that as Griffin sat in the cockpit he looked straight down the flight deck. The elevated tail was Pennoyer's idea and was done so that the Vought would already be in flying position at the start of its roll.

Griffin switched on the magneto booster, yelled "Contact!" and a sailor swung the propeller. The Wright engine kicked over, blue smoke belched from the exhaust stacks, and the propeller faded into a whirling blur. Wheel chocks held the plane in place during the warm-up, but the real test would come when Griffin revved up the 180-horsepower engine all the way. To hold the plane down, Pennoyer had built what he called a "tension gun." The device was a steel cable attached to a deadeye in the deck and clipped with a quick-release hook to the plane. A trip wire on the hook was held by a sailor off to the side of the plane.

Satisfied that everything was ready, Griffin shoved the throttle forward to full power. The plane bucked and shook, straining to break free of the tether as the chocks were jerked away. Looking straight ahead, Griffin nodded his head once, and the operator jerked the hook release. Tail up, at full power, the little plane shot forward and was airborne before it even reached the elevator. Elated, Griffin climbed, rolled, and swept down across the deck. Everyone on deck was cheering and waving as he roared over and banked away toward Norfolk. Carrier aviation had been launched in the U.S. Navy.

Getting an airplane off the deck was one thing, but getting one back on was another. The problems were formidable. The *Langley* had an arresting system designed by Lieutenant Mel Pride, a reserve officer who had studied at the Massachusetts Institute of Technology. Pride's design was an adaptation of one used by the British. It consisted of a complicated arrangement of twenty-two parallel steel cables that ran fore and aft and four cables that ran athwartships.

The twenty-two fore-and-aft cables resembled the strings of a violin, spaced a foot apart. They were held eighteen inches above the deck by two "fiddle bridges," one at each end of the cables. Those cables, intended to guide the plane down the flight deck in a straight line, would be snagged by steel hooks on the plane's axle. A long hook, lowered by the pilot from the plane's fuselage, was designed to grab one of the four athwartships cables and stop the plane's forward progress.

The *Langley*'s very narrow deck, and her tendency to roll, made the problem more difficult. Additionally, the absence of shock-absorbers in the landing gear meant that the plane had a strong tendency to bounce back into the air after a hard landing, increasing the danger that the pilot might lose control and go over the side. The fact that no U.S. Navy pilot had ever landed on the deck of an aircraft carrier, under way at sea, was the least of the problems.

In October 1922, Lieutenant Commander Godfrey de Courcelles Chevalier ("Chevvy" to his friends) took off from Norfolk and headed out over the water toward the *Langley*. He found her just inside Cape Henry, steaming at six knots into a thirty-knot wind. Chevalier made a pass down the flight deck, noted that the white landing flag was hoisted, and curved around to make his approach.

More than a half century after the event, it is difficult for us to imagine the problems that faced Chevalier during that first carrier landing. There were absolutely no landing aids, there was not even a landing signal officer. He was flying an Aeromarine 39-B trainer, powered by a Curtiss OXX-6 engine rated at 100 horsepower. There were not more than six instruments on the dash, and the fixed landing gear was virtually without any sort of shock absorbers. His landing place was a narrow ribbon of wood, rolling and pitching sixty feet above the water, and moving forward at six knots. Starting at the after end of the flight deck, the wire maze, intended to trap his plane and keep it on the deck, extended just 200 feet forward. A gust of wind or poor timing would put Chevalier down on the deck forward of the arresting gear—and into the drink. Poor timing could also reduce his wood and canvas plane to kindling at the after end of the flight deck.

Chevalier started down toward the *Langley*, nose up, hook down. On the flight deck the arresting wires quivered in the wind. Spec-

Lieutenant(jg) Chevalier makes the first landing on the *Langley* in an Aeromarine, 26 October 1922. (Photo courtesy of *Naval Aviation News*)

tators and deck hands waited in the netting slung along the edges of the flight deck. As the Aeromarine came in, its right wing dropped. Chevalier brought it back up. The plane roared over the end of the deck, its hook catching the second wire. The plane slammed down, and Chevalier cut the power as the axle hooks grabbed the fore-and-aft wires. As the plane was jerked to a wrenching halt, its tail upended, smashing the propeller on the wooden deck. U.S. carrier aviation had arrived.

On Saturday night, 28 October, the *Langley* pilots had a wild celebration at the Norfolk Yacht Club. Understandably, Godfrey Chevalier was the star of the evening, and his fellow pilots presented him with a silver cup to commemorate his milestone accomplishment. Tragically, Chevalier died two weeks later in a crash ashore that was caused by an incompetent ground crewman.

The last test to be conducted before the *Langley* began her full-scale experimental operations was to catapult a plane from her deck. Catapult launchings from cruisers and battleships were commonplace in 1922, but the system used aboard the *Langley* was

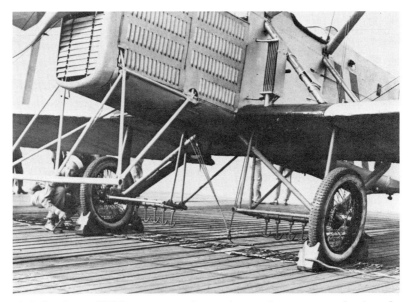

Axle hooks on DT-2 were part of arresting equipment on early aircraft. Corrugated metal fiddle bridges extend under the plane's tires. (Photo courtesy of *Naval Aviation News*)

different. Instead of a turntable, the catapult was built into the deck and was designed to hurl a heavily loaded plane off the end of the flight deck. The executive officer, Commander Whiting, assigned himself to the job.

The plane chosen for the test was a Naval Aircraft Factory (NAF) PT torpedo seaplane. Even in 1922 the PT looked like a relic that belonged in a museum. It was, in fact, constructed of war-surplus parts. Why a seaplane was chosen for the catapult test is not clear. Considering the obvious problems involved, it would seem that a wheeled plane such as the VE-7 would have been a better choice. But, for whatever reason, the PT was picked, and the decision nearly cost Whiting his life.

Jackson R. Tate, a *Langley* pilot at the time, recalled that in order to launch the PT the

> . . . twin-float seaplane was set on a remarkable carriage mounted on castors, . . . built by the ship's force. The carriage was set on deck and attached to the catapult traveller. The pontoons were locked to the carriage by hooks which were released at the end of the catapult run, when they were hit by a trigger sticking up from the deck.[10]

On 18 November 1922, Whiting climbed into the cockpit of the PT and started the engine. Running the twelve-cylinder Liberty to full power he gave the signal to fire, and the Rube Goldberg

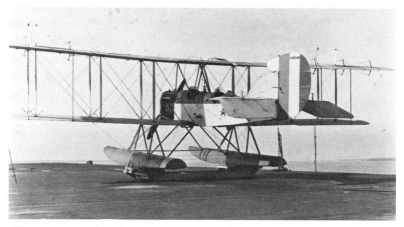

The PT secured to its launch carriage sits on deck. The aircraft was a composite of WW I parts. (Photo courtesy of *Naval Aviation News*)

contraption lurched forward. Gaining speed, the plane started to lift, raising the right pontoon and its carriage off the deck. The plane shot across the triggers, uncoupling the left pontoon and carriage, but missing the right. Free of the weight on the left, but encumbered by the still-attached right pontoon/carriage assembly, the PT rolled to the right as it flew off the end of the flight deck. Whiting was in real trouble, when suddenly the right pontoon sheared off and tumbled into the sea with its firmly affixed carriage. Whiting righted the plane and flew off with only one pontoon. Whiting's problems were not over. He still had to land. Bringing the crippled plane in carefully he set her down on the remaining pontoon, and then hung on while she slewed in alongside a crash boat. Both Whiting and the plane were returned to the *Langley* at the end of what Tate described as "a somewhat unusual start for air operations."

The initial tests completed, the *Langley* started the serious business of developing a new form of naval warfare. Because the British were so secretive about their own efforts, the Americans had, essentially, to develop carrier aviation from scratch. For the next thirteen years, the *Langley* developed equipment, tested ideas, and trained the pilots who would go to the big, fast attack carriers then building.

Crashes were common in the early years, and Commander Whiting had started the practice of filming each landing so that the pilots could review and study what had happened. He had the films edited, separating the good landings from the bad landings. In a short time the "disaster films" greatly outnumbered the good.

Some of the crashes resulted from equipment failure, but most were caused by the absence of any sort of landing aid. Jackson Tate recalled:

> Up until this time, each pilot was strictly on his own, and various types of landing approaches were employed. Mel Pride, the man who made the most and the best landings, used a slow-turning, flat approach with the nose high and using power. This was finally accepted by all pilots and became standard.[11]

The solution to the landing aid problem came about almost by accident. When not flying, Commander Whiting stood on the after port corner of the flight deck, watching the planes land. As each plane came in, Whiting would unconsciously make hand and body motions that reflected his view of the plane's approach. His "body language" was so explicit that many pilots responded to the "signals" that Whiting unconsciously made with his hands. Whiting's unintentional motions resulted in the creation of the landing signal officer.

But there were still problems with the arresting gear that would not be entirely cleared up until 1929. The most common occurrence was for a plane to hit the deck, lunge forward, and then fall on its nose. Little real damage was done to the plane, but the wood deck soon began to look like a chopping block. The sequence was also hard on propellers.

A partial solution was to build what amounted to a bumper in front of the landing gear. The *New York Times* described the problem, the cause, and the solution:

> During the early flights of the *Langley* several planes were thrown forward violently on their noses, smashing their propellers, but doing no major damage to the machines. This tendency, . . . has been corrected by placing a small wooden frame between the fuselage and the top of the landing wheels. When a plane tips forward on landing on the *Langley*'s deck this frame touches the deck and the pull of the weights below causes it to immediately assume an upright position.[12]

Throughout her years as an aircraft carrier, landing operations were an exacting, dangerous, and exciting event. As Charlie Bolka recalls:

> Those were the days of the fore and aft cables. My forty-man crew was kept scrambling during air ops, insuring that they were properly aligned. There were four cross-deck wires that were attached to cables that ran along both sides of the flight deck. Those two cables ran down to the bottom of the ship to "cages." There was a man stationed at each cage. As each plane came in, the air operations officer decided how much weight was needed for that particular plane, and I passed the word to the men at the cages. Their job was to select the proper weights for each plane and attach them to the cables.[13]

When a plane swept across the end of the flight deck, the men standing in the nettings along both sides of the deck ducked. The hook caught the arresting wire, the cables along each side of the deck whipped and raced aft, and fiddle bridges crashed down. George Van Deurs was standing in the nets one day in 1926.

> I stood in the nettings and watched her take a squadron of fighters aboard. At that time someone beside me said, "Those aren't landings. They're barely controlled crashes!"[14]

As the basic techniques improved and more planes were brought aboard, the forward deck was often crowded with parked planes. By 1925, a pilot who missed the wires was faced with the prospect of plowing into a dozen parked aircraft. To reduce this possibility, a rope barrier—something like a tennis net—was strung across the deck, forward of the landing wires.

By that time, the *Langley* had launched and recovered all the wheeled aircraft in the Navy's inventory. As new types were introduced, they too were modified for carrier landings and sent out to the *Langley*. Receiving a new aircraft was both a thrill and a potential disaster. Typically, the deck and nettings were crowded with onlookers and factory representatives. Bolka recalls that in these instances:

> . . . occasionally an aircraft landed faster than expected, and a barrier engagement loomed. In order to prevent that unhappy occurrence, a manually operated brake on each cable was activated. This brought the plane to an abrupt, jarring halt. But a couple of times the aircraft's hook remained on the wire while the aircraft continued into the barrier. Factory tech reps were not amused.[15]

In 1925, a "Lieutenant Flagg of VF-2" landed on the *Langley* in a much more sedate but wholly unacceptable manner. Flagg was making a routine practice pass down the flight deck when

> . . . by premeditation he landed and brought his plane to rest in the middle of the deck near the elevator where the arresting gear was not rigged. . . . His engine was idling when he came to rest. Wind about thirty-three miles over the deck. Said he had always wanted to try it.[16]

Earlier that same year, Lieutenant H. J. Brow had made the first, though unofficial, night landing aboard the carrier. On the night of 5 September 1925, Brow was making practice passes in

Between March 1920 and March 1922 the *Jupiter* was transformed into the *Langley* (CV-1). The *Jupiter* had spent just eighteen months on the West Coast, but as the *Langley* she spent nearly eighteen years in the Pacific. This picture taken in San Diego in 1934 shows her in her salad days. The cruiser in the background may explain why eight years later a Japanese pilot mistook one of her escorting destroyers for a cruiser. (Photo courtesy of Earl Dixon)

preparation for the real thing scheduled for the 8th. Brow had just cleared the after end of the flight deck when his aircraft "stalled" and plopped down onto the deck. Whether accidental, or simply because, like Flagg, he "always wanted to try it," Brow was the first to make a night landing aboard a U.S. carrier.[17]

Slowly, through trial and error, the *Langley*'s pilots and crew were establishing a workable, efficient system. Some of their early solutions to problems proved to be unworkable. But in at least one case they were able to convert failure into something useful. Because the planes had no radios, homing pigeons were brought aboard to carry messages from the planes back to the ship. According to Jackson Tate, "the attempt to train pigeons to return to a ship was a great failure, but provided an excellent supply of squab for the mess."[18]

In 1936 the *Langley* was assigned as a seaplane tender to the Commander Aircraft Base Force in San Diego. Her days as an aircraft carrier were over. There was a touch of irony to the assignment. In 1919 and 1920 when the advocates of the aircraft carrier were arguing for a chance to test their ideas, the supporters of seaplanes and flying boats were their strongest rivals. With the commissioning of the *Langley* the decline of the seaplane started, although few people realized it at the time. Then in 1936 the progenitor of modern carrier aviation became the servant of the group it had made obsolescent.

31 March 1934. The *Langley*'s planes are ready to take part in a demonstration for President Roosevelt. (Photo courtesy of Grant Squire)

With her aircraft tied down and ready for sea, the *Langley* prepares to get
under way. This photo shows how narrow the flight deck was. The line
across the deck in the foreground is not an arresting cable. Just behind
that is the elevator, along the forward edge of which the flight deck was
cut off in 1936. During takeoffs and landings, the radio mast in the background was unshipped, leaving an unobstructed flight deck. (Photo courtesy of Grant Squire)

Five weeks after her reassignment, the *Langley* headed toward
Mare Island Navy Yard near San Francisco for modifications that
would make her a more useful seaplane tender. On 25 October
1936, one day short of the fourteenth anniversary of Chevalier's
first landing, she launched two airplanes. They were the last airplanes that ever flew off her deck. That afternoon she entered
Mare Island Navy Yard.

The modifications made on the *Langley* included cutting off
the flight deck back to the forward edge of the elevator, shortening
the deck about 41 percent. Her remaining flight deck became a
convenient place to park flying boats for transport or to work on
them. Eight fueling stations were added along her main deck, and
holds that had previously been converted from coal bunkers to
aircraft hangers and workshops became living quarters and spare
parts storerooms. Her bridge was modified by the addition of an
open signal bridge that spanned the original structure but did not

Shorn of 41 percent of her flight deck, America's first aircraft carrier took up her less glamorous duties as a seaplane tender in 1937. Despite her reduced status she was probably the finest seaplane tender in the world, and this photo illustrates why. (National Archives)

rise above the flight deck. Six months later she was redesignated AV-3 and the conversion was complete.

She was assigned to the Aircraft Scouting Force tending seaplanes out of Seattle, Sitka, Pearl Harbor, and San Diego. On 27 May 1937 the *Langley* steamed under the newly completed Golden Gate Bridge. It was opening day and her passage beneath the spectacular bridge symbolized her new status—she was the second ship to pass under the span after it had been officially opened.[19]

For two years she serviced flying boats between the West Coast and Hawaii, attracting little attention. Then in May 1939 she popped briefly into the limelight as one of the naval attractions at the New York World's Fair. A colorful brochure giving a brief history of the ship concluded with the statement, "Twenty-seven years of hard service as a collier, aircraft carrier, seaplane tender. Even yet there is plenty of life left in the good old Langley."[20]

The writer who prepared the brochure, and the happy people who flocked aboard the tender, could not have dreamed that the *Langley* would be sunk thirty-three months later. Upon assignment to the United States Asiatic Fleet, the *Langley* again headed for the West Coast, and obscurity.

The *Langley*'s flight deck as it appeared after her conversion to AV-3, when it became a convenient storage area for cargo and equipment. This picture taken in 1938 probably shows the tender en route to Pearl Harbor. The aircraft on her deck are Consolidated P2Ys. (Photo courtesy of Eugene Eckstein)

There are, however, former crewmen who say that her two years in the Asiatic Fleet were her best. She had been a good test bed, and a less than mediocre fleet carrier, but she was probably the best seaplane tender to serve in any navy before the war. Her truncated flight deck provided a spacious work area, an aircraft parking lot, and a recreation field. Her galley was one of the finest in the Asiatic Fleet, and her crew accommodations were among the best. She is remembered by her former crewmen as "a happy ship."

The good life ended abruptly on 8 December 1941. The *Langley* was anchored in Manila Bay, off Cavite, when the Japanese made their simultaneous attacks on Pearl Harbor, the Philippines, and Malaya. That evening the *Langley* led two tankers, the USS *Pecos* (AO-6) and the USS *Trinity* (AO-13) out of Manila Bay, past Corregidor, and south toward the Netherlands East Indies. It was not a headlong flight but an orderly withdrawal, during which the *Langley* tended PBYs of Patrol Wing Ten, and the *Pecos* fueled the scattered elements of the Asiatic Fleet.

The *Langley* tending flying boats at Sitka, Alaska, in 1937 or 1938. Six of the planes on the water are PBYs. The seventh, on the far left, is a P2Y. (Photo courtesy Eugene Eckstein)

It was clearly evident to the men in the three ships that the war was off to a bad start. As the convoy headed south, the Japanese were already advancing down the Malay Peninsula and pushing through the Philippines. No relief was coming from Pearl Harbor, and the Japanese were out in overwhelming force. By mid-December the three ships had avoided all contact with the enemy, and their crews had not yet been under fire. But the situation was tense and the men were jumpy.

As the three ships were steaming south across the Sulu Sea between the Philippines and North Borneo under a clear tropical sky, the *Langley*'s four 3-inch antiaircraft guns suddenly opened up. Startled sailors on the *Pecos* and the *Trinity* searched the sky for the *Langley*'s target. On the flight deck near the sand-bagged fire control center, a warrant officer, Gunner H. E. Anderson, heard a sailor say that the target's angle of elevation was not changing.[21] Squinting at the silver dot in the sky, Anderson saw why. Several hundred yards away on the bridge of the *Pecos*, Commander

E. Paul Abernethy, who had taken a sandwich from his Filippino mess boy, also saw why.

"Captain, who for *Langley* shoot at Venus?" asked the bewildered Filippino.[22]

Commander Abernethy laughed. Like Gunner Anderson, he saw that the *Langley*'s target was the planet Venus. The incident became a standing joke, with the *Langley*'s crew laughing as hard as anyone else.

Wryly, Commander Abernethy commented that it was "good pointer drill even though there really was not enough ammunition for interplanetary target practice." But Michel Emmanuel, a young reserve ensign on the tender, successfully defended his ship's honor when he pointed out that the *Langley*'s navigator "brought Venus down."[23] In fact, the incident was a humorous preview of tragic events to come, when the *Langley*'s rounds would again fail to reach the target.

CHAPTER 2

The Plan

During the three months following the Japanese attack on Pearl Harbor, the Allied defense of the Southwest Pacific was marked by disorganization and confusion that resulted from several causes. The most important was the lightning speed southward of the Japanese advance, which in terms of time and distance was more dazzling than the often-lauded German blitzkrieg in western Europe. (Between 8 December 1941 and 9 March 1942, the Japanese completed a 3,000-mile advance, or about 230 miles per week. The blitzkrieg lasted about six weeks and accomplished a westward thrust of about 600 miles, or about 100 miles per week.) The result was that the Allies were always off balance—a condition that was compounded by a lack of inter-Allied coordination.

In the early weeks of the war, the Japanese were essentially fighting three separate enemies: The United States; Great Britain (including Australia); and the Netherlands. But in early January 1942, at about the time that the *Langley* arrived in Darwin, the three Allies tried to coordinate their war efforts by forming what was supposed to be a unified command, designated ABDACOM (American-British-Dutch-Australian Command).

The immediate goal was to hold the Malay Barrier formed by Malaya, Sumatra, Java, Lesser Sunda Islands, and Australia. Field Marshal Sir Archibald Wavell became the supreme commander, with Lieutenant General George H. Brett, USA, as his deputy. Command of the combined, Allied naval forces (ABDAFLOAT) was given to Admiral Thomas C. Hart, USN. The land forces were commanded by a Dutch lieutenant general, and the air forces by a British air marshal.[1]

On paper the organization looked good, but in reality it suffered from many shortcomings. Among them were operational stumbling blocks resulting from language differences, logistics problems caused by the many different types of equipment used by the four Allies, and a qualitative and quantitative inferiority in aircraft. Additionally, there was a lack of coordination between the air and naval arms, a circumstance that was reflected in the muddled plans that sent the *Langley* on her last mission.[2]

The Japanese, by comparison, did not suffer from disorganization or a lack of coordination between their air and naval arms, and air power was the dominate feature during their thrust south. From the start they had attained and held air superiority, an advantage that resulted, generally, from two factors.

The first factor was the geography of the area, which allowed them to fight along short, interior lines. This advantage, unusual for an attacker, enabled the Japanese to construct a network of captured and newly constructed airfields rarely more than 300 miles apart.[3] This meant that they could quickly concentrate their air power locally in overwhelming numbers. The second factor was the long range and superior quality of the A6M (Zero) fighter.

The importance of air power to the successful defense of the Malay Barrier was emphasized in an ABDACOM directive issued to Field Marshal Wavell on 3 January 1942. In the directive he was told that "the first essential is to gain general superiority at the earliest moment through employment of concentrated air power. The piece-meal employment of air forces should be minimal."[4] The key to air superiority in this instance was the fighter plane, for without fighters the Allies could neither stop the Japanese bombers nor protect their own weak bomber forces.

By the time that directive had been issued, even the remotest possibility that ABDACOM might achieve air superiority had become a pipe dream. Effective Allied air strength in the first half of January 1942 was a pittance compared to what the Japanese could muster. Not only was the number of airplanes on hand small, but most of the Allied planes were either obsolescent or completely outclassed by the Japanese. The Allies' first-line fighters, the Hawker

Hurricane and the Curtiss P-40, were no match for the Zero, but in the hands of an experienced, trained pilot both planes had at least a chance of survival. Unfortunately, there were far too few Hurricanes and P-40s available, and still fewer trained pilots.

But Japanese air power was not winning the war alone. While the Japanese 25th Army was pushing through Malaya toward Singapore and the 14th Army was slugging it out with the Americans in the Philippines, the Japanese prepared a three-pronged attack intended to seize the oil-rich Netherlands East Indies. The right prong, designated the Western Force, was to move south from Camrahn Bay (Indochina) and take objectives on South Sumatra, Bangka, and Palembang, thus setting up an attack on western Java. The center prong, designated the Central Force, was to start from Davao (Philippines) and roll down on Tarakan, Balikpapan, and Bandjarmasin, opening the way to invade Java from the east. The left-hand prong, designated the Eastern Force, also was set to jump off from Davao and follow a route immediately beside the Central Force. In fact, the two prongs were so close together that they essentially formed one striking force. The Eastern Force was responsible for the seizure of Manado, Kendari, Ambon, Makassar, Timor, and Bali, nearly all of which represented important air fields that would extend Japanese air superiority south and cut off reinforcements to Java from Australia.

A special Java Force was to be held back until the three prongs secured their last objectives. Then the Java Force would move south from Camrahn Bay and Davao to make the main landings on western and eastern Java. The date for those landings was set for 28 February.

At the time the formidable Japanese plan was put in motion, the newly formed ABDACOM was just getting organized. On 10 January Field Marshal Wavell arrived in Java and established his headquarters in Lembang at the island's western end. That same day the Central Force seized Tarakan in northern Borneo, and the Eastern Force secured Manado in the Celebes.

As the Japanese advance pushed into the outer areas of the Netherlands East Indies, the Allies were frantically trying to find fighter planes with which to reinforce the already decimated front-line units. The only unit immediately available was the 17th Pursuit

Squadron (Provisional) that had been hastily put together with veterans of the Philippine fighting and was issued the only flyable P-40s in Australia.[5] On 16 January the squadron left Brisbane en route to Java with seventeen P-40s in the first attempt to beef-up

ABDACOM's main line of resistance around the Malay Barrier.

ABDACOM's dwindling fighter forces. The planes were flown in stages across Australia to Darwin, a distance of about 2,000 miles. From Darwin they made another series of hops along a 1,600-mile route across Timor, Bali, and Surabaja to Blimbing.

Seventeen planes were hardly enough to meet ABDACOM's needs for the defense of the Malay Barrier, and plans were pushed forward to send more. The urgency to reinforce Java was heightened by the heavy losses suffered almost at once by the 17th Pursuit Squadron and by the speed at which the Japanese were closing in on their final objective. In late January the Americans and the British were still willing to give their all in the defense of Java, and a second batch of planes was scraped together and readied for the flight across the Indian Ocean.

While those efforts were being made, the Japanese plan continued to move forward like clockwork. Balikpapan fell on 23 January, Kendari on the 24th, Pamangkat (Dutch Borneo) on the 27th, and Ambon on 1 February. The capture of Kendari made it possible for Japanese bombers to reach Timor and eastern Java, and coupled with the seizure of Ambon, it was evident that the Japanese would shortly move against Timor and Bali. When those islands were taken, the air corridor from Australia to Java would be closed.

Kendari and Ambon had already been occupied by the Japanese when the second attempt was made to fly fighters into Java from Australia along the Darwin-Surabaja air corridor. The second group sent out was formed from recently arrived provisional squadrons, the 3rd and the 20th Pursuit Squadrons, plus part of a dive-bomber outfit, the 91st Bombardment Squadron. Those three units represented the only other attempt to reinforce Java by air after the 17th Pursuit Squadron had been sent across. Between 29 January and 11 February the three green squadrons made the long trip from Brisbane to Surabaja, losing 60 percent of their planes along the way. By the time they reached Blimbing, they had ceased to exist as fighting units, and the remnants were absorbed by the already badly battered 17th Pursuit Squadron. The replacements brought the 17th's strength up to an all-time high of twenty-six fighters.[6] But twenty-six fighters were hardly enough, and the Army planners started looking for more fighters that could be sent forward.

Immediately available were two intact and partially equipped pursuit groups—the 35th, training at Sydney, and the 51st, which was due to arrive in Melbourne on 1 February. Those units, and the 51st group's thirty-three crated P-40s, could be reloaded into four contract transports and dispatched to Java shortly after the 51st arrived in Melbourne. Also immediately available were two green pursuit squadrons, the 13th and the 33rd, in Brisbane. Their P-40s were already assembled.

The ABDACOM planners were faced with three basic requirements: they had to obtain as many fighters as possible; the planes had to be made combat ready in the least amount of time after their arrival; and losses en route had to be kept to zero. Satisfying the first requirement was limited by the number of P-40s immediately available in Australia. The second requirement stemmed from the need to assemble the crated aircraft after they arrived in Java, and the third requirement obviously resulted from the high losses experienced in the two attempts to fly P-40s into Java.

By the end of January it became evident to ABDACOM planners that continuing the ferry flights to Java would result in unacceptable losses, due mainly to pilot inexperience. They also recognized that it was only a matter of time until the Japanese captured Timor, after which ferry flights would be impossible. Around 5 February the Army planners began to develop an idea for sending ready-to-fly fighters to Java by sea. The plan that took shape was marked by confusion, which largely resulted from a lack of communication between all the headquarters involved.[7]

By 10 February ABDACOM had determined that thirty-two ready-to-fly P-40s from the 13th and 35th Pursuit Squadrons could be transported to Java aboard the *Langley*. The planes would fly from Brisbane to Fremantle and be put aboard the tender. It appears that the initial plan called for their delivery to Surabaja on the island's east end. But the Japanese had been bombing the huge navy base on a daily basis since 3 February, so that a need for an alternate port already existed. Therefore, the decision on which port to use was left open.[8]

Orders were issued directing the *Langley* to move down to Fremantle and take aboard thirty-two P-40s. At the same time, the 35th and 51st Pursuit Groups were loaded aboard Convoy MS-5

The *Langley*'s mission was to deliver thirty-two ready-to-fly P-40Es to Java. It was a desperate gamble that failed. (U.S. Air Force photograph)

in Melbourne and sent around the bottom of Australia to Fremantle. All the elements—Convoy MS-5, the thirty-two P-40s, and the *Langley*—were scheduled to come together in Fremantle and depart together for the same, as yet unannounced, destination in Java.

The first hint of confusion surfaced when the movement orders were issued. Major Homer "Tex" Sanders, commanding officer of the 51st, assumed that the thirty-two P-40s to be transported aboard the *Langley* were to become part of his group.[9] First Lieutenant William Keenan, a veteran of the Philippine fighting and commanding officer of the scratch squadron, believed his planes were intended to bolster the 17th.[10] It was also unclear whether the *Langley* was to be a part of Convoy MS-5 after leaving Fremantle or just attached to the convoy for the trip across.[11]

On 11 February thirty-six P-40s took off from Brisbane en route to Port Pirie where they would receive additional instructions before flying on to Fremantle. Thirty-six planes were sent with the hope that at least thirty-two would reach Fremantle. The precaution was justified, since except for Lieutenant Keenan, most of the pilots had little or no experience with the P-40s. From the start of the flight they had problems that included getting lost, mechanical failure, and landing accidents that resulted in the 2,400 mile trip across Australia requiring six days to complete.[12]

The *Langley* left Darwin on the same day, sailing down Australia's west coast toward Fremantle. The following day at 1630

The routes the three elements took to Fremantle, Australia.

Convoy MS-5, carrying the 51st and 35th Pursuit Groups, departed Melbourne en route to Java via Fremantle. The convoy, escorted by the cruiser USS *Phoenix*, was made up of two American freighters, the SS *Holbrook* and the SS *Sea Witch*, plus two Australian freighters, the SS *Duntroon* and the SS *Katoomba*. The *Holbrook* and the *Katoomba* carried the bulk of the 51st, and six of its P-40s aboard the *Holbrook;* the 35th was aboard the *Duntroon*. The *Sea Witch* was carrying the "major portion of the airplanes," twenty-seven; all the 51st Group's jeeps and trucks; and nearly three quarters of a million rounds of .50-caliber ammunition for the planes.[13] It appears from the documents that the 35th may not have been supplied with fighters, which may have been the case owing to the shortage of P-40s in Australia at that time. Thus the *Sea Witch* became the most valuable ship in Convoy MS-5, as events ten days later were to show.

As the ships steamed out of the harbor, eleven of the P-40s that had left Brisbane on the previous day flew over the convoy.

The unintentional event prompted Major Sanders to write in his diary:

> 4:30 P.M. 2nd phase of our odyssey begins. Away from the pier at Melbourne and into the harbor. A few minutes later 11 P-40s flew over on way from Brisbane. To me, they are a symbol of the might which we will eventually bring into being to crush the life from the Japanese. I wonder if our men know what we are sailing into. Some are offering 2:1 that we don't make it.

The pessimism about the Java situation expressed in the major's diary was widespread throughout the Allied headquarters in Java and Australia. When Sanders had been briefed on the mission by Colonel Ross Hoyt on 6 February, Sanders was told that none of his group was expected to come back. Colonel Hoyt's prediction reflected growing British and American doubts that Java could be defended.

Despite the growing doubt, plans were still being made to further beef-up the island's fighter strength. While Lieutenant Keenan and his green pilots were flying toward Fremantle, General Brett sent a message from Java to Army Air Force Headquarters in Australia saying that:

> *Langley* should arrive Fremantle approx. February eighteenth. Load there two hundred and fifty enlisted men, fifty officers, full complement P-40s. Send sufficient pilots and mechanics to fly aircraft from unloading location NEI. If necessary send additional squadron personnel to fill out organizations already sent to convoy. Plan to use Fremantle for similar future deliveries. Hold all other squadrons in southern area for possible carrier transportation. Send two pursuit squadrons to Darwin. *Langley* shipment first priority after fighter squadron for Koepang. *Atheae* en route Australia due Fremantle approx. Feb. sixteenth and Melbourne twenty-second to load crated P-40s. She carries forty-nine partially dismantled Hurricanes. Load and return ship to NEI. Investigate and advise possibility sending crated P-40s Perth for erection or transshipment in crates. You will be advised of further requirements.[14]

The message was confusing since steps to load the *Langley* with thirty-two planes and pilots had already been taken. Where the 300 officers and enlisted men were to come from is a mystery, and what he meant by a "full complement" of P-40s is unclear. Certainly he did not intend that the officers and enlisted men were to come from the 51st and 35th Groups, since he had also ordered additional personnel to fill out those units if necessary. There is also the question of where 300 men were going to find space aboard the *Langley*. The general's message was an example of the confusion that resulted from a lack of communication between the various staffs and headquarters involved. The situation was destined to become worse.

As the three elements moved toward their meeting in Fremantle, events were taking place that deepened Allied pessimism. On 14 February the Japanese Western Force landed troops near Palembang, Sumatra, close to the western tip of Java. That same day a change of command occurred in the ABDA organization that sealed the *Langley*'s fate. Admiral Hart was replaced by a Dutch officer, Vice Admiral Conrad Helfrich, as ABDAFLOAT. The situation in Java was deteriorating rapidly when Admiral Helfrich took command of ABDAFLOAT, and his English-speaking allies at Supreme Headquarters were about to reach the decision to pull the plug in Java. Their decision was hastened when on 15 February Singapore fell, thus securing the Japanese flank and opening the way for the two-pronged attack on Java.

That same day Vice Admiral William A. Glassford, Commander U.S. Naval Forces S.W. Pacific (COMSOWESPAC) and deputy of ABDAFLOAT, moved his administrative headquarters from Surabaja to Tjilatjap. The move was made because daily air raids "made it increasingly evident that Surabaja would soon be untenable as a base for surface ships."[15] It was also apparent that the Japanese would soon make their move for Bali, and when they did Surabaja would be closed. It was now even more important that an alternate port be designated to receive Convoy MS-5 and the *Langley*.

The following day the Allies received lessons in how effectively the Japanese controlled the waters and skies around the island and how fruitless it was to attempt sending reinforcements by sea without air cover. On 16 February a convoy heading for Timor, the vital stepping-stone along the air corridor, was attacked by Japanese aircraft and driven back to Darwin. Gloom deepened at Supreme

Headquarters in Lembang, and the first of several changes in plan occurred that clouded the *Langley*'s mission.

On 17 February, when Convoy MS-5 was still one day away from Fremantle, General Brett apparently decided that sending the convoy to Java was a waste of men and planes, not to mention ships, and he changed the convoy's destination from Java to India.[16]

As the deputy to Field Marshal Wavell, General Brett was in a position to issue orders that went out as ABDACOM directives. It was, however, an advantage that could only be used sparingly. In this case he was acting in America's best interests, since he believed that Java was lost and that the war should be continued from bases in India and Australia. The field marshal agreed completely with that view and thus had no objection to Brett's essentially unilateral decision.[17]

By agreement, any ABDA member nation could appeal an ABDACOM order issued to one of its units if the member felt that the order was contrary to its own best interest. Any American appeal went to Chief of Staff General George Marshall in Washington. Though Marshall subscribed to the principal of unified command, he allowed his line commanders a wide latitude of independence.[18] Inasmuch as General Brett was one of the originators of the plan to bring Convoy MS-5 and the *Langley* to Java, and his decision to change the plan was supported by his superior, there was no need for him to contact Washington. Had he done so, Marshall would undoubtably have supported him. Thus, in this instance, General Brett had a pretty free hand to do what he thought best. But when the Dutch were notified of the change in plan, they were outraged and protested heatedly. The sensitive issue was not where the convoy was being sent, but where the convoy's planes were being sent. Altogether there were sixty-five P-40s in Convoy MS-5 and aboard the *Langley*. This meant that if all the ships stayed together, they would arrive somewhere with sixty-five fighters. Therefore, when the Dutch learned that the convoy's destination had been changed from Java to India, they were outraged over the loss of all those airplanes.

It is significant that Brett's order applied only to Convoy MS-5 and did not mention the *Langley* and her thirty-two P-40s. He may have assumed that the tender was included in Convoy MS-5, and therefore special orders regarding the ship were unnecessary. But it is doubtful. Navy movement orders did not include the *Langley* as a part of Convoy MS-5, and apparently orders went directly to the ship from COMSOWESPAC. Brett probably knew that and was more concerned with saving two established fighter groups, consisting of several hundred men, than he was about saving a scratch squadron of thirty-two green pilots.

That reasoning is not as cold-hearted as it sounds. By rerouting only Convoy MS-5, he would be withholding two valuable organizations for future use and fulfilling his commitment to ABDA-COM with the *Langley*'s less valuable group. Additionally, since the Dutch were determined to make a stand in Java no matter what happened to ABDACOM, the *Langley*'s thirty-two ready-to-fly P-40s were the quickest means of providing the Dutch with some sort of fighter cover. Therefore, no matter what disposition was made with respect to Convoy MS-5, the *Langley* was still routed to Java.

Since the tender and her thirty-two ready-to-fly planes were not affected by Brett's order, the Dutch protest really centered on the *Sea Witch* and her cargo of twenty-seven crated P-40s. As a result of the Dutch protest, a decision was made to detach the freighter from the convoy and have her accompany the *Langley* to Java.[19]

At the same time, change and confusion were also present in the orders sent to the operations officer in Port Pirie regarding the P-40s assigned to the *Langley*. The group had already been broken up, some of the planes having been reassigned to Darwin. Replacements for the reassigned planes were being flown in from Brisbane when the harried operations officer was told:

> That thirty-two operational P-40s be placed on USS *Langley* is imperative. Not more than thirty-six are to be dispatched beyond your station. That the four additional spares will be enough to ensure that thirty-two operational P-40s are loaded aboard this carrier is hoped. We repeat you are ordered to dispatch four additional P-40 aircraft beyond Port Pirie so that you are able to put aboard USS *Langley* by February eighteenth thirty-two aircraft that must be aboard her. Objective is known to you and if necessary dispatch more than four additional planes beyond Port Pirie.[20]

On 17 February thirty-three P-40s landed in Fremantle, but one flown by Second Lieutenant J. P. Martin cracked up on landing. Lieutenant Martin, nevertheless, decided to go on board the *Langley*

The Japanese three-pronged assault on Java was launched from French Indochina and the Philippines. By 27 February 1942 all three prongs had reached their final objectives and were ready to enter Java.

with his friends, despite the fact that the orders only called for thirty-two pilots and planes.[21] It was a fatal decision.

The following day, 18 February, Convoy MS-5 plodded into Fremantle just a few hours behind the *Langley*. That same day a large Japanese convoy departed Camrahn Bay, followed by a second convoy from Jolo on the 19th. Protected by ten cruisers, thirty-one destroyers, and an aircraft carrier, ninety-six transports packed with men and equipment of the 16th Army were headed for Java. The bell had rung for the final round.

As the Japanese moved in for the kill, ABDACOM sorted out the plans for Convoy MS-5 and the planes, and notified Army Air Force headquarters in Melbourne about the change. Melbourne replied to ABDACOM that the routing changes had been made, but the message showed that there was still a lack of communication regarding the new plan:

> Instructions are being given to the *Phoenix* in accordance with your 403 A to sail with *Holbrook Katoomba* and *Duntroon* to Burma area (port to be designated later) under convoy of *Phoenix* as soon as ready to put to sea. Request you communicate to us or to *Phoenix* direct port of debarkation. *Sea Witch* is being given orders through commanding officer *Phoenix* to report to commanding officer USS repeat USS *Langley* for instruction. We assume here that you have issued instructions direct to *Langley*.

During the night of 21–22 February the thirty-two P-40s that had been flown across Australia were towed through town to the dock where the *Langley* was tied up. The method used to move the fighters ten miles through town was as makeshift as was the plan to deliver them to Java. The tail of each P-40 was tied to the bed of a truck, and the plane was pulled from the airfield to the dock. Because of a manpower shortage, the pilots drove the trucks while a scratch crew of ground crewmen from the 51st Group rode on the tailgates to be sure that the planes and trucks did not part ways.[22]

The following morning the *Langley*'s air officer, Lieutenant Commander Harry Hale, had the Army planes hoisted aboard and tied down. Twenty-seven were parked on the flight deck; the remaining five were crowded onto the main deck, beneath the flight deck. Later that morning, the pilots went aboard accompanied by twelve crew chiefs from the 51st Group. Shortly after the enlisted men had gone aboard, another change was made and they were recalled. In their place went twelve crew chiefs from the 35th Pursuit Group whose names, in the last minute confusion, were not recorded. For the men of the 51st Group, the exchange was fortunate. For the men of the 35th it was a death sentence.[23]

On 19 February, even before the P-40s had been loaded aboard the tender, Darwin had been bombed and reduced to a smoking ruin, and Bali was being taken. The next day Timor fell and the Darwin-Surabaja air corridor was cut. But the most ominous development occurred on Bali. Immediately after it was secured, elements of the Japanese Navy's 11th Air Fleet, including the Takao Air Group, began operations from those newly acquired airfields. Situated close to Java's eastern tip, those air units effectively closed the sea route from Australia to Java.

By the time Bali had been taken, American and British pessimism had hardened into the firm conviction that Java's days were numbered. On that day General Brett began evacuating Allied civilians, and on the 20th he reported to Washington his intentions to evacuate Army Air Force personnel.[24] But the plans for the *Langley* remained unchanged. She was scheduled to sail for Java on 22 February.

In the meantime, as a result of the deteriorating situation in which Surabaja had become unusable, a decision had to be made as to which port the *Langley* and the *Sea Witch* could enter. Admirals Glassford and Helfrich discussed the matter shortly before the ships were scheduled to leave Fremantle. Admiral Glassford recalled:

> There was much discussion as to the port of entry of these two plane-carrying ships. Tjilatjap was eventually decided upon and preparations at that port were made most hurriedly accordingly. There was no flying field at or near Tjilatjap. The planes were to be unloaded on the dock and then towed along the streets to a comparatively open field and from there flown to various flying fields for operation against the enemy. The plan was a makeshift one rendered necessary by the hazard of using either Batavia or Surabaja, both of which were being subjected to continuous air bombing during daylight. Much had to be accomplished at Tjilatjap for the reception of the planes. Streets had to be cleared and material and gear had to be rearranged on the

pier in order that the planes might be landed and towed away safely. Up to this time Tjilatjap had suffered no serious bombing. Hopes ran high. The labor situation was serious as the great majority of native laborers had taken to the hills at the first indication of bombing.[25]

Both ships were scheduled to arrive in Tjilatjap on 28 February—the date set by the Japanese for the invasion of Java.

CHAPTER 3

The Crossing

At noon on 22 February while an Australian Army band played "Farewell to Thee," the *Langley* departed Fremantle with Convoy MS-5, escorted by the cruiser USS *Phoenix*. Shortly before departure the *Sea Witch*'s skipper had reported to the *Langley* for special orders and learned that his ship would be joining the *Langley* on her unescorted run to Tjilatjap. Aboard the SS *Holbrook* Lieutenant Colonel Sanders, celebrating his three-day old promotion, still thought he and his group were headed toward Java.

Thus, the plan to reinforce Java by sea that had started with two pursuit groups plus the additional airplanes, pilots, and mechanics on board the *Langley*, had been reduced to just the *Langley*'s cargo, and finally ended with a compromise that sent the planes carried by the *Langley*, plus those carried by the *Sea Witch*, to Java without the two pursuit groups.

To confuse the enemy, the plan called for the *Langley* and the *Sea Witch* to leave Fremantle on the 22nd with the convoy and head for India. Then on the 25th, near the Cocos Islands, the two ships would break away and head for Tjilatjap. The last 120 miles, the most dangerous stretch, was to be covered during the night of the 27th, with arrival at Tjilatjap set for early morning on the 28th.[1] Inasmuch as the Japanese had firmly established air superiority around Java, a night approach was the only real defense the ships would have during the final run in.

But on the evening of the 22nd Admiral Helfrich (ABDA-FLOAT) changed the plan and ordered the *Langley* to break away from the convoy that night and make a lone dash toward Tjilatjap.[2] By that time, according to Admiral Glassford, there were not more than fifteen fighters in all of Java. Thus, the shortage of aircraft was so severe that the Dutch were desperate for the *Langley's* ready-to-fly P-40s. The ship's new arrival time was set at 0930 on the 27th, which meant that she would still make her run into the coast under cover of darkness. The *Sea Witch* stuck to the original schedule.[3]

When these orders were sent to the *Langley*, Admiral Glassford, whose responsibility included the seaplane tender, was unaware of them. In fact it was not until much later that the Dutch admiral told the American what he had done.[4] Expressing regret to Admiral Glassford that the orders had been sent directly to the ship rather than routed through him first, Admiral Helfrich explained that "time was the most important factor" and that he had taken that "liberty to save time."[5] He may also have believed that had he not taken the liberty of issuing a direct order, the *Langley* might never have gone to Tjilatjap.

By 22 February relations between the Dutch and their allies were not smooth. The Dutch had been very unhappy with the choices made for the top staff positions with the ABDA organization, in which only one Dutch officer had any real responsibility. Inasmuch as the Netherlands East Indies were the key to the ABDA defense area, and the Dutch were the most knowledgeable about the area and the sea around it, they felt they should have had more responsibility for decisions regarding its defense.[6]

Admiral Helfrich was particularly unhappy with the setup, and complained that until he replaced Admiral Hart as ABDAFLOAT on 14 February he had no direct contact with ABDACOM in Lembang. Despite the fact that he commanded the Dutch naval forces in the East Indies, he claimed that he was never asked for advice, and only found out about Allied plans through the Dutch naval officer assigned to the ABDACOM staff.[7] Whether or not his complaints were fully justified is a matter of opinion, but the fact is that he and other Dutch officers felt they were being pushed aside.

The incident also provided an example of the lack of coordination between the Army Air Force and the Navy. Until Admiral Helfrich stepped in and issued orders directly to the *Langley*, Glassford apparently believed that both the *Langley* and the *Sea Witch* were bound for Ceylon.[8] Up to that time all the decisions made regarding Convoy MS-5 and the *Langley* had come from ABDACOM through General Brett, and it appears that ABDACOM was not passing all the information on to Admiral Glassford at COMSOWESPAC. From the way Admiral Helfrich handled the *Langley* matter after his appointment to ABDAFLOAT, it appears he also limited the information that his headquarters gave the American naval commander.

General Brett's apparent failure to communicate all the facts to Admiral Glassford may have been an oversight that resulted from the confusion that attends a deteriorating military situation. But Admiral Helfrich probably deliberately withheld information from Glassford. The Dutch knew the British were planning to pull out of Java, and they could hardly have been unaware that the American Army Air Force was following suit. The only organization that had not openly supported the assessment of the situation made by Wavell was the U.S. Navy. But under the circumstances, Helfrich had to assume that the Navy's commitment was, at best, shaky. What Helfrich did not know was that despite preliminary moves away from Java, the American Navy was going to honor its commitments to ABDACOM even if everyone but the Dutch pulled out.

It is not surprising, therefore, that Helfrich used his newly acquired authority as ABDAFLOAT to divert the *Langley* ahead of schedule without consulting Glassford. Admiral Helfrich also knew that if Glassford found out about the order early enough to have it countermanded, he could appeal the order to General Marshall in Washington. If that was his reasoning, Admiral Helfrich had misjudged his American subordinate. When finally informed, Admiral Glassford fully supported the change.[9]

Obedient to the orders from ABDAFLOAT, the *Langley* hurried along toward Tjilatjap at her best speed, about 13 knots. For her own safety it was imperative that she keep the new schedule and arrive off Tjilatjap at about dawn. As a further precaution, before dawn on the 27th she was to rendezvous with two American destroyers, the USS *Edsall* (DD-219) and USS *Whipple* (DD-217), which would provide an antisubmarine escort into the harbor. As she steamed north, confusion and misunderstanding that resulted from a lack of clear communications between the various headquarters again surfaced on 23 and 24 February. Though the misunderstanding had no effect on the change in plans made before the ships left Fremantle, it illustrates how fouled up things were.

The reader will recall that the *Sea Witch* had been reassigned to the Java mission as a result of the Dutch protest over the ship being rerouted to India. Subsequently, Army Air Force headquarters in Melbourne notified ABDACOM that the *Sea Witch*'s captain had reported to the *Langley* for special orders. Apparently, Melbourne did not know what those special orders were, though that is hard to imagine. In any event, on 23 February they sent a message to ABDACOM that said in part: "UNDER PRESENT ORDERS THE SEA WITCH IS PROCEEDING TO INDIA ACCORDING TO UNDERSTANDING OF THIS HEADQUARTERS."[10]

The following day, ABDACOM, replied: "NECESSARY TO DIVERT *SEA WITCH* TO NEI TO UNLOAD 400,000 ROUNDS OF .50-CAL IN ORDER TO SUPPLY AMMUNITION FOR PLANES ON LANGLEY."[11] Clearly there were people in Melbourne and ABDACOM who had lost track of the game plan.

As the *Langley* steamed alone toward Java, ABDACOM was falling apart. The Army Air Force had already started its withdrawal, and on 23 February Admiral Glassford learned that the British were also pulling out. On the 25th Field Marshal Wavell withdrew to India and ABDACOM for all practical purposes ceased to exist. Vice Admiral Helfrich assumed overall command of the meager remains and was assured by Admiral Glassford that the United States Navy would remain, a commitment for which Admiral Helfrich was "profoundly grateful."[12] Despite the practical dissolution of ABDACOM, the *Langley*'s mission remained unchanged.

Admiral Glassford's assurance to Admiral Helfrich was the result of orders from the Commander in Chief U.S. Fleet "substantially to report for duty to . . . Helfrich."[13] Glassford had no illusions about the situation and probably would have fallen back to Australia had he enjoyed the same freedom of action that General Brett did. The senior British naval officer, Rear Admiral A. F. E. Palliser, was similarly bound to stay, but with orders to "withdraw the British naval forces from Java when further resistance in his judgement served no useful purpose."[14] Admiral Glassford did not enjoy even that option.

Thus on 26 February, the *Langley* and the *Sea Witch* were committed to a mission that had little hope for success and would in no way delay the inevitable outcome of the Japanese assault on Java. There was still time to recall both ships and send them on to India where their cargo would be vastly more useful. But that could not happen because the Army had apparently written off the fifty-nine planes, and the Navy was committed to a policy of standing by the Dutch until the end. Hence there was no one who would countermand the existing orders. In any event, it would have been impolitic not to have made some effort to satisfy the Dutch need for fighter planes. But without a doubt, any effort made at that late date was futile.

By 26 February, almost daily changes in the plan for getting the *Langley* to Java had become a routine feature of the mission. It was, therefore, no surprise when at 1300 two Dutch PBYs were sighted, and one reported that the tender's escort was already twenty miles to the west. The *Langley* changed course, losing valuable time, and met the Dutch minesweeper *William Van der Zaan* instead of the two American destroyers.[15]

The Dutch minesweeper proved to be even slower than the *Langley,* whose captain, Commander Robert P. McConnell, was not at all pleased with the situation. If he stayed with the Dutch ship, his arrival in Tjilatjap would be delayed several hours, which would mean that his ship would lose the protection from air attack afforded by the planned night run to the coast. The security of darkness and an escort of two American destroyers were a lot more attractive than the escort provided by the minesweeper, and the *Langley* left the Dutch ship behind.

Several hours later McConnell received an order from Admiral Glassford's headquarters confirming that the *William Van der Zaan* and the two PBYs were to escort the *Langley* to Tjilatjap. It was an odd order, because returning to the *William Van der Zaan* would throw the already altered schedule out the window. Faced with no alternative, the *Langley* put about and headed back toward the Dutch ship.

Commander Robert P. McConnell, skipper of the *Langley* on 27 February 1942. Though his actions were fully justified, poor report writing almost got him into serious trouble. (Photo courtesy of Lawrence Divoll)

But the *William Van der Zaan* had hardly come into view when another message was received ordering the *Langley* to turn around again and rendezvous with the *Whipple* and the *Edsall* as originally planned. Steaming over the ground she had covered twice already, the *Langley* plodded back toward Tjilatjap. On the bridge, the skipper fumed at the stupidity of the conflicting orders that had cost so many precious hours. Instead of arriving in Tjilatjap in the early morning, her new arrival time was set for 1700.[16] Obviously there would be no protective cloak of darkness for the old tender as she crossed the last 100 miles to Tjilatjap. Instead, her passage would be made in broad daylight, while well within range of the Japanese bombers on Bali. Commander McConnell radioed his new arrival time to COMSOWESPAC and requested air cover.

Admiral Glassford was aware of the added danger the *Langley* now faced and wanted to delay her entry into Tjilatjap until the morning of the 28th—the original schedule before all the changes were made. Glassford discussed his recommendation with Helfrich who turned it down. In his report Glassford recalled that:

> ..., the situation of the *Langley* was brought to the attention of Vice Admiral Helfrich. The time of her predicted arrival at Tjilatjap was discussed in detail. He confessed time was the all important factor. He wished that she should not be delayed until the following morning to enter with the *Sea Witch,* thus permitting both to approach the coast under cover of darkness. He said to me repeatedly that the responsibility was his alone; that he must get those planes in and at the enemy; that every minute counted. There had been no bombing off the south coast of Java and 5:00 P.M. was too late for enemy bombing of Tjilatjap itself. He even asked me to inform the Commander in Chief U.S. Fleet that he took full responsibility . . . I could not permit him to take this stand alone as I did in fact share completely his views as to the necessity for taking the risk and subscribed fully to his decision.[17]

The only thing left to do was inform McConnell that there would be no air cover.

At 0700 on 27 February the *Langley* met her escorts, and after a brief detour to avoid a submarine proceeded toward her still-distant goal, flanked by the old four-pipers. Two hours later, when she should have been entering the Tjilatjap Channel, she was spotted by a Japanese patrol bomber, one hundred miles short of her goal.

After the patrol plane had disappeared, the three ships plowed across the deep blue water under fair tropical skies, every available eye searching the horizon for the bombers that each man knew were coming. Standing on the navigation bridge, Commander McConnell had feelings of anger and defeat. From the start he and his officers had known that the mission had little practical hope of success. After the Japanese reconnaissance plane found the *Langley,* what faint hope existed had been erased. McConnell, an exceptionally practical man, knew that only a miracle could save his ship and her mission. But in February 1942 Allied miracles were on back order.

It was ironic that the ship that had pioneered the aircraft carrier concept in the U.S. Navy and had played a major role in defending naval aviation against the contrary efforts of General William "Billy" Mitchell had entered a combat zone loaded with planes she could not launch and which belonged to the Army. In a remote sense she had again become the handmaiden to a former detractor. The irony continued with historical reference to an immediate concern. The *Langley* had pioneered the type of warfare that made it impossible to operate surface ships near the enemy without air cover, a fact that had been recently demonstrated by the loss of HMS *Repulse* and HMS *Prince of Wales*. Yet the *Langley*, an ex-aircraft carrier and in effect a reminder of the new type of warfare, was in a combat zone in which the enemy had complete air superiority. Without air cover and possessing only ineffectual antiaircraft armament, she had, as her executive officer, Commander Lawrence Divoll said, "no business being there."[18]

The patrol plane had raised some fears, but apparently only a handful of crewmen gave serious thought to the fact that the *Langley* was entering a combat zone in which she was virtually defenseless. It would be a misrepresentation to say that any of them were completely unconcerned about having been spotted by the patrol plane, but most of them seem to have been generally optimistic. That was in part due to their trust in their officers and in part to the belief most young men have in their own invulnerability. But the biggest factor in their optimism was probably the fact that none of them had been in combat. Still, the patrol plane was anything but encouraging, and it appeared that most of the crew adopted a wait-and-see attitude about what would happen next.[19]

There were, however, men who were concerned about what might happen during the next three or four hours. Their concern was based on previous experience, and information that had come to them during the course of their duties. Radioman Second Class Bernard Jasper, an ex-gunboater who had seen the Japanese in China, had been in the radio room on the night that the *Langley* had been ordered to break away from the convoy. Since that time, strict radio silence had been observed and general quarters drills had been stepped up. Jasper was certain that very soon one of those alarms would be the real thing. He had voiced his opinion to the warrant officer in charge of the radio room.

Radio Electrician Charles A. Snay agreed with Jasper, but his agreement was based on stronger evidence than Jasper offered. Young, bright, and energetic, Snay had spent much of his time since leaving Fremantle at his post in the crypto room. When not there he was usually on the bridge studying navigation under the tutelage of Lieutenant Commander W. W. Soule. As a result of those lessons, Snay was one of the few people on board the ship who was aware of the consequences posed by the multiple changes in plan.

Jasper's prediction and Snay's agreement did not worry two young second-class radiomen, David Jones and Bill Warnes. Since leaving Fremantle, they had been kept busy lugging heavy batteries back and forth between the P-40s and the charging rack. The work was particularly hard on Jones whose right hand, broken in horseplay with Warnes, had not yet completely mended. The job was nearly finished, and only a few batteries remained to be installed on the morning of the 27th. Neither man suspected that the job would not be finished.

Machinist's Mate First Class Jim Harvey was another sailor who gave little thought to the growing danger, though as a gunboater he had also seen how the Japanese operated before he was transferred to the *Langley* in October 1940. Unlike Jasper's spectator role, Harvey's experience with the Japanese had involved a face-to-face confrontation on a baseball diamond.

Harvey was the star pitcher on the ship's championship baseball team. Before joining the ship, he had played the same position on a less successful team of gunboaters on the Yangtze. One afternoon shortly before being sent to the *Langley,* the gunboaters were playing a Marine team when a company of armed Japanese soldiers suddenly moved onto the field. The soldiers, ostensibly on a training exercise, started digging positions and setting up tents on the field.

The Americans protested angrily, but the Japanese ignored them and continued what they were doing. Irate at the impudence and arrogance, the Americans took up baseball bats and threatened to crack Japanese heads. The explosive situation was moving rapidly toward the ignition point when an American officer intervened. The officer may have been intent on preventing a nasty international incident, but more likely he was saving American lives. The Japanese were obviously prepared to use bayonets and bullets against ball bats.

But Harvey did not compare that experience to the situation that was building around him. Jim Harvey had a philosopher's eye for viewing events, and he saw the interruption of that baseball game by the Japanese as symbolic of the interruption of his life by the war. What bothered him on 27 February 1942 was that he had never been able to go back and finish the ball game, and he wondered if the same might be true of his life.

Considerably less philosophical was big, affable Thomas Spence. The jovial seaman first class was calculating the probability of getting liberty in Tjilatjap, and though he had heard no official word, he believed that liberty was a near certainty. He based his opinion on the fact that as one of the captain's orderlies he had not heard any officer say there would be no liberty granted.[20] His opinion was supported by his good friend Seaman First Class Roy "Breezy" McNabb. In Breezy McNabb's opinion, it would take as long to unload the fighters in Tjilatjap as it had taken to load them in Fremantle. There had been ample liberty granted in Fremantle, and McNabb saw no reason why the same would not be true in Tjilatjap. Spence agreed with McNabb's logic.

Breezy was particularly enthusiastic about the subject of liberty and was speculating on the availability of Dutch beer. Spence was equally enthusiastic, but had some reservations about McNabb's big spending plans. Breezy made a practice of pawning Spence's wrist watch to bankroll their adventures, and though he had always managed to reclaim the watch before the *Langley* sailed, Spence was not altogether sure that his luck would last forever.

Three other close friends were too busy to think about liberty or what might happen now that they had been spotted. They were the *Langley*'s three bakers for whom a seven-day work week was standard procedure while the ship was at sea.[21] The eldest was a slightly built, red-headed Irishman, Baker First Class Joseph F. Riley. Good natured and patient with his two youthful assistants, Riley was nevertheless inflexible on how things should be done in the galley. He had been in the Asiatic Fleet for nearly twenty years, was married to a Filippino girl, and had a child. The word that the ship had been spotted by a Japanese reconnaissance plane had no effect on Riley, who had no thought for his own safety. He was worried sick, however, that the Japanese might have already killed his wife and baby.

Baker Second Class Robert McLean was the youngest of the three friends but had been in the navy four years longer than his giant friend, Baker Third Class Frank Wetherbee. McLean, a handsome ladies' man and a scrapper, had once suggested that he could whip any man in the ship except Wetherbee. The baker second class may have been overly optimistic on the first point but he was undoubtedly right about the second. Wetherbee, an enormously strong ex-logger, was one of the strongest men on the ship.

Between those who saw the discovery by the patrol plane as a sign of impending disaster and those who ignored it, was a small group of men who viewed the expected result with a technical eye. Among them was Electrician's Mate Third Class Lester Bates, who had only been a part of the *Langley*'s crew for six weeks. Bates was a tall, lanky twenty-year-old who made friends easily, probably because of his cheerfulness and unlimited optimism.

Since leaving Fremantle, Bates had been working beneath the flight deck installing permanent phone cables and power lines for the ship's primitive fire control and gunnery system. Bates' had heard the gunners say that the *Langley*'s antiaircraft defenses were next to worthless, but he did not pay much attention. He did notice, however, that one good hit would take out nearly all of the ship's communications system.

Seaman First Class James Saulton was another newcomer aboard the *Langley,* and like Bates he was part of a crew working to improve the 3-inch antiaircraft guns on the flight deck. The guns, mounted on pedestals, had not been provided with splinter shields when they were installed in Cavite before the war. On the run south from the Philippines, the guns had been encircled by sandbags in an effort to afford some protection to the gun crews. Since leaving Fremantle, Saulton and the others had been using boiler plate and sheet metal to build forms around the guns, filling the space between the forms with cement to make better splinter shields. The job had been finished on the afternoon of the 26th, and for Saulton the work had special meaning—he was a loader on the number-two gun.

Gunner's Mate Third Class Reginald Mills was one of the gunners that Bates had heard talking. Mills had no faith in the effectiveness of the *Langley*'s 3-inch guns against an air attack. In fact, he was convinced that if the airplanes came low enough, there was a better chance of downing one with the four .50-caliber machine guns that were mounted on the bridge. Looking forward, the gunner could see two 5-inch "bag guns" intended for defense against other ships. The guns on the bow, and two more like them on the stern, would have no role to play if the *Langley* were attacked from the air.

The useless 5-inch guns were commanded by two reserve ensigns who had joined the *Langley* early in 1941. Ensign J. R. Asdell was responsible for the forward pair and his good friend Ensign Michel Emmanuel was stationed aft. Asdell's thoughts about what was to follow are not available, but Ensign Emmanuel was wondering if fate had finally caught up with him.

Commissioned in 1941, he was sent to the Asiatic Fleet with orders to go aboard the minesweeper USS *Penguin* at Guam. One of his classmates, Ensign Walter Senschuck, was also being sent to the Asiatic Fleet, but with orders for the *Langley*. For personal reasons the two officers arranged to trade assignments—Senschuck to the *Penguin* and Emmanuel to the *Langley*. On 8 December 1941, the *Penguin* was sunk and Senschuck ended up in a Japanese prison camp. At the time, however, Emmanuel believed that his friend had been killed and that the trade had saved his life. On 27 February, Emmanuel was thinking that his luck had only been temporary.

Yeoman Third Class John Kennedy was another man aboard the *Langley* who was wondering what hand fate had dealt him. Kennedy, a reservist, had come into the Navy as an arson investigator with Naval Intelligence. En route to Guam when the war started, his ship had been diverted to Sidney, where it was discovered that Kennedy had both a private pilot's license and a college degree. The combination apparently impressed someone as being the ideal requirement for assignment to the *Langley*, and on 10 January 1942 Kennedy joined her in Darwin. The assignment looked good to him, because he thought it might open the door to a transfer to naval aviation. On 27 February, however, his chances for a transfer were starting to look dim.

It appears that the Army Air Force personnel aboard the *Langley*, like the sailors, had mixed reactions about the patrol plane. But there was one feeling about which there was complete agreement among the airmen, and which may have been strengthened by the sighting. They all wanted off the ship. Typical of the feeling was the sentiment expressed by Second Lieutenant Gerald J. Dix.

Since Pearl Harbor had been bombed, Dix seemed to have spent all his time either at sea, on the ground in Australia, or just waiting. He had earned his wings in September 1941, but so far he had spent only seventeen hours in the cockpit of a P-40, and most of that had been logged on the flight to Fremantle. He was tired of ocean crossings, tired of waiting, and eager to fly in combat.[22]

Therefore, his assignment to the *Langley* mission had been greeted with enthusiasm, despite the planners' bleak prophecy that none of them were expected to come back. Undoubtedly, the Army planners were thinking about what would happen when the green pilots tangled with the veteran Japanese. As it worked out, Dix and his fellow pilots never got into the air, but the planners were about 97 percent accurate anyway.

Among those who clearly recognized the significance of the patrol plane, the captain and his executive officer were the most concerned. Commander Robert P. McConnell was a tall, blond, ruggedly handsome officer, who had dropped out of the University

Commander Lawrence Divoll, the *Langley*'s very popular executive officer. (Photo courtesy of Lawrence Divoll)

of California at Berkeley to become a naval aviator during World War I. Thorough and conscientious, he had survived the draconian manpower cuts following the war, earned a regular commission, and had moved steadily up the promotion ladder. His executive officer, Commander Lawrence Divoll, was a competent and dedicated officer—firm, but compassionate, and independent to the point of being mildly unorthodox. He knew almost every man on the ship by name, and their problems were his.

Shortly after the patrol plane flew off, the captain told Divoll that he thought something about the impending danger should be said to the crew. Divoll agreed, and McConnell told him to handle the matter. Under a brilliant blue tropical sky studded with altocumulus clouds, an ideal setting for a peacetime, commercial cruise ship, Divoll's voice, unexpectedly serious, boomed out over the ship's loudspeakers:

> Boys I'm just a little bit scared. We're going to catch hell and I want everybody to concentrate and do his job. I wish you all the best of luck.[23]

The speaker clicked-off, and five hundred young men suddenly realized that today might be forever.

•

CHAPTER 4

The Attack on the *Langley*

1150–1158

"*Whipple* signaling aircraft sighted!"

The excited shout turned every head toward the destroyer that was already maneuvering to avoid attack. Binoculars swept the sky to the east, focusing on several small dots that were silhouetted against the scattered altocumulus clouds.

"Sound general quarters."

Throughout the ship, bells, gongs, and horns sent men scrambling for steel helmets and running to their battle stations. Watertight doors slammed shut, antiaircraft guns trained around toward the oncoming enemy, and ammunition handlers began passing ammunition from the forward 3-inch magazine along a human chain to the guns.

Having given the order to sound general quarters, the captain hurried up a ladder to the signal bridge, an open area atop the bridge structure. From that position he had an unobstructed, 360-degree view and could communicate via voice tube with the navigating bridge. With him on the bridge were thirteen men, including two Army pilots; Lieutenants William Akerman and Gerald Dix, who had been acting as lookouts. The other men were his talker, his gunnery officer, Lieutenant Walter Bailey, and nine machine gunners.

McConnell, watching the Japanese bombers through his binoculars, saw them swing around from a point off the *Langley*'s starboard quarter to a position dead astern. The bombers were still several miles away but were closing rapidly at about 15,000 feet. From his left he heard his talker say, "All guns report manned and ready."

"All guns" represented very little with which to defend the ship. The *Langley*'s antiaircraft armament consisted of four 3-inch guns mounted on the flight deck, four .50-caliber machine guns mounted on the four corners of the signal bridge, and a few men spotted around the ship with Browning Automatic Rifles (BARs).

The BARs, designed for use by infantry as a squad support weapon, were worthless in an antiaircraft role. The .50-caliber machine guns could only be effective if the attackers came within a few hundred feet of the ship, and their effectiveness depended primarily on massed fire—two conditions that could not be expected to develop during a high-level attack.

The 3-inch guns appeared to offer the best hope for beating off an attack. But it was a false hope. The guns, a World War I

The Browning Automatic Rifle (BAR) was actually an infantry squad weapon, but was used aboard the *Langley* and the *Pecos* as an antiaircraft weapon. It was useless in that role, and typified the inadequacy of antiaircraft armament aboard U.S. ships during the early days of World War II. (National Archives)

The Lewis gun was a drum-fed, light machine gun that had first been used in an airplane in 1912, and was widely used on the ground and in the air during World War I. Like the BAR, it was not suited to the role of an antiaircraft gun, but during the early days of World War II it was about all there was. The Kelly helmet, or "tin-hat," worn by these two gunners is the type that was worn aboard the *Langley* and the *Pecos* during the attacks. (National Archives)

development, could only reach targets up to about 12,000 feet. Additionally, their slow rate of fire—in the *Langley* about four rounds per minute for each gun—and the absence of an adequate fire control system, reduced their effectiveness to almost zero.[1]

The *Langley*'s fire control center was a circle of sandbags located on the flight deck in the middle of the four guns. Inside the circle were Ensign Lanson Ditto, his talker, Yeoman Third Class Kennedy, and two sailors. The sailors operated a jury-rigged device that was a post with a sighting bar at the top. The post could be rotated 360 degrees, and the sighting bar could be elevated from horizontal to 70 degrees. At the base of the post was a brass ring graduated in degrees with a pointer that protruded from the post. When the post was turned, the pointer indicated the target's relative

The Browning water-cooled, .50-caliber, heavy machine gun was used throughout the war as an antiaircraft weapon. But unless the guns could be grouped in batteries to achieve massed fire, they were only marginally effective. The *Langley* had only four of these guns, and the *Pecos* had ten. This picture was taken aboard the USS *Enterprise* (CV-6) in February 1942. (National Archives)

bearing from the ship. Below the sighting bar was a brass quadrant, also graduated in degrees and equipped with a pointer. When the sighting bar was elevated, the pointer showed the target's angle of elevation. While one sailor operated the sighting bar and rotated the post, the other sailor read the angle and bearing and reported them to the officer, and Kennedy passed the information on to the gun crews via telephone.[2]

The four 5-inch guns, two on the forecastle and two on the stern under the flight deck, were intended for defense against surface attack and had no antiaircraft capability. They were, nevertheless, manned during the attack.

Watching the bombers grow steadily larger in his lenses, Commander McConnell knew that his ship was ill equipped for the battle he had hoped to avoid. The *Langley*'s only real hope lay in whatever ability she had to outmaneuver the bombers. "Commence firing," he ordered.

On the flight deck Ensign Ditto heard the order repeated by John Kennedy, who hardly had time to put his headset on before

The 3-inch × 50 antiaircraft gun was a World War I development that was virtually ineffective during World War II. It simply did not have the range nor the rate of fire needed to knock down more modern aircraft. The *Pecos* had two of these guns mounted amidships and the *Langley* had four mounted on her flight deck. The *Pecos* got hers when she was built, but the *Langley*'s were added at Cavite in 1941. (National Archives)

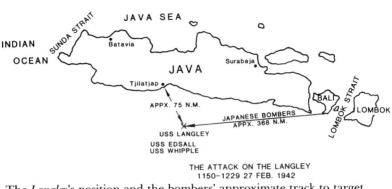

THE ATTACK ON THE LANGLEY
1150-1229 27 FEB. 1942

The *Langley*'s position and the bombers' approximate track to target.

the order was given. A ragged volley launched the tender's defense, followed by slow but steady firing from each gun. The *Langley*'s guns were joined by those from the destroyers, and soon the clear tropical sky was splotched with black flak bursts.

Measured by the smooth, purposeful activity taking place at each gun, the defense looked impressive. As each gun fired and recoiled, its breech opened spilling a hot, spent case onto the deck. Quickly a gloved hot-shellman scooped up the case and tossed it over the splinter shield. A loader shoved a new shell into the breech, the trainer and pointer traversed and elevated the barrel, tracking the target, and the gun captain pulled the firing lanyard.

"Bridge wants to know what fuse settings you're using," Kennedy said to Ditto.[3] The ensign could see that the rounds were exploding well below the bomber formation. He was not surprised. Since the bombers had been sighted, Ensign Ditto had been steadily estimating the altitude, speed, and target angle of the approaching formation. From the beginning he had known that the planes were beyond the range of his guns. To Ditto, the smooth team work exhibited by the gun crews was both impressive and commendable—but a waste of effort.

"Maximum," he answered. Ensign Ditto's estimate of the situation was correct on every point. 15,000 feet overhead, Lieutenant Yoshinobu Tanabata led his seven-plane squadron in on the bomb run, undisturbed by the angry, black flak bursting several hundred feet below his plane. Tanabata's squadron was formed up in two three-plane Vs, one behind the other, with the seventh plane tucked in behind the second V. Each plane had a 551-pound (250-kg) bomb shackled to the bomb rack beneath the fuselage, and Tanabata's plan was to drop all seven bombs in salvo.[4]

The approach was flawless, every plane rock steady, the formation tight. Tanabata concentrated on the plane-covered *Langley* directly in front of his squadron, completely uninterested in the escorting destroyers. His bombardier lay prone in the nose, peering through a simple sighting device, hand-gripping the mechanical bomb release lever. Tanabata saw the after edge of the *Langley*'s flight deck slide beneath the bomber's nose, and felt his plane lurch upward as the bombardier pulled the bomb release.

"NERK NERK V 1MCZ BT AIR AIR RAID RAID" flashed from the *Langley*'s radio mast as the seven bombs hurtled down.[5] Whether a warning, a report, or a plea for help, there was nothing the listeners could do.

On the signal bridge, Commander McConnell was trying to estimate the bomber's point of release by gauging the angle of elevation. More importantly, he hoped to be able to see the bombs fall from the aircraft. But by the time the angle of elevation had reached 80 degrees, he had still not seen any bombs drop, and he decided that he could not wait any longer.[6]

"Hard right rudder!" he bellowed down the voice tube. On the navigating bridge the officer of the deck repeated the order, and the helmsman spun the wheel. The *Langley* heeled to port, her hull skidding broadside along the original course as the bow swung around. She was halfway through her turn when Tanabata's seven-bomb salvo struck the water. Had McConnell delayed another second before making the turn, his ship would have been squarely under the bombs.[7]

All seven bombs struck the water along the tender's original course, with a thundering explosion that churned the sea and threw up tall columns of water. But the *Langley*'s narrow escape was not complete. Two bombs exploded in the water close to the ship's side, sending out shock waves that slammed into her hull with the force of a freight train. The blow split seams, buckled plates, and sent rivets flying across the ship's interior. Tons of water poured through the openings.

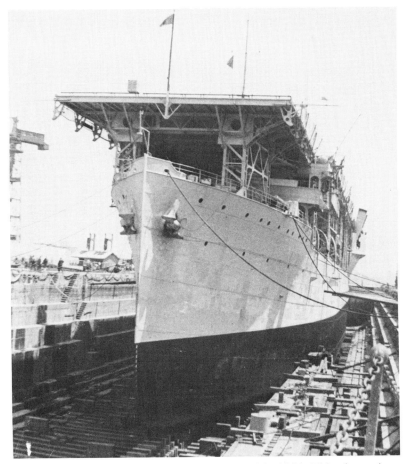

The *Langley* (CV-1) in dry dock at Mare Island in 1934. This picture is a good view of the hull along the port side and shows the area below the waterline that was hard hit by the near-misses. The first two near-misses exploded near the funnels and opened several seams below the waterline. Radiomen David Jones and William Warnes were sitting against the hull at about where the first shoring timber is in this picture. Shrapnel from a third near-miss penetrated the hull forward of the shoring timber and almost to the anchor, narrowly missing Jones and Warnes. (Photo courtesy of Grant Squire)

As the bombs fell toward the ship, many men were still running toward their battle stations. Someone shouted "take cover" just before the bombs hit, and men dropped flat on the deck. Seaman

First Class James Mealley had been running along the port side when he felt the ship maneuver radically and heard the shouted warning. He threw himself down just as the twin geysers erupted from the sea accompanied by a loud roar. Suddenly there was a tremendous booming noise and he bounced several inches off the steel deck. As the columns of water collapsed in a shower of spray and foam, Mealley jumped up and ran to his place among the 3-inch ammunition handlers.

In the steering engine room, Machinist's Mate First Class Millard McKinney felt the ship "shake like a dishrag," accompanied by a deep rumbling noise. Forward on the port side, Radioman Second Class Jones heard the clatter of shrapnel against the hull and felt the ship lurch under his feet. Jones was lucky. A few feet forward of his position, shrapnel penetrated the hull.[8] The experience momentarily frightened the men, but then everything seemed to return to normal, and they dismissed it.

Deep in the ship's hull the engine room crew had been most affected by the two near misses. One of the bombs had gone off right alongside the engine room, and the shuddering blow to the hull had knocked half of the men off their feet. The sledgehammer-like shock wave ruptured water lines, smashed castings to sea connections on the fire and bilge pumps, and shattered several fire-mains. Instantly the men were drenched by seawater that sprayed from dozens of holes and broken connections. But the water spewing from the damaged piping was a mere nuisance compared to the discovery that was made as the bruised crewmen got back on their feet—water was rising in the bilges.

With water rising in the bilges the *Langley* was already facing a potentially serious problem. The problem was due to the fact that her two electric motors were mounted in the lowest point in her hull, essentially in the bilge. Each motor stood inside its own, open box-like structure. The walls of the boxes were about six feet high and were intended to keep any water that ran into the bilges from reaching the motors. This meant that the bilges could be flooded to a depth of about five or six feet before the water would reach the top of the walls and pour into the motor pits.[9]

Once the motor pits started to flood, the *Langley* would be in serious trouble. When the water depth in the motor pits reached three or four feet, the electric motors would have to be shut down to prevent what was described as an "electric explosion."[10] When the water rose above four feet, the motors themselves would be flooded out, and there would be no hope of restarting them. Without power the *Langley* would be helpless, and in a combat zone an immobile ship was doomed.

When the flooding in the bilges was first discovered, the water was rising slowly and there was no immediate threat. But the bilge pumps, due in part to the many ruptured lines, could not keep up with the steady rise, and unless the flooding could be controlled the *Langley* was finished.

Frantically Machinist F. E. Butts, assisted by two brothers, Chester and Norman Koepsell, worked to plug the leaks. Rubber patches were slapped over the holes and held in place with wire or rope. Within fifteen minutes they had the situation under control and the pumps appeared to be holding their own against the in-rushing water. There were still many leaks to patch and lines to be rerouted, but if things stayed as they were, Butts and his men were confident that the situation could be kept in hand.[11]

The engine room situation was reported to the bridge with the additional information that there did not appear to be any way to stop or reduce the flooding. The damage control officer, Lieutenant Commander Thomas Donovan, confirmed the latter point, adding that his men had not been able to locate the exact source of the flooding. Since the crew could not reduce the inflow of water nor increase the pump's capacity to pump it out, survival depended on maintaining the delicate balance between flooding and pumping. There were only two variables and neither could be expected to go in the *Langley*'s favor. The best to be hoped for was to maintain the status quo. The reports disquieted McConnell.

While the captain listened to the gloomy situation report, and the engine room crew struggled to keep up with the inflowing water, the 3-inch ammunition party was steadily passing ammunition to the four guns on the flight deck. The human chain began in the forward magazine deep in the ship's hold, where ammunition was passed up in wooden boxes, two shells per box. The chain extended up to the main deck, snaked through the tightly packed P-40s to the break at the poop, and then up to the boat deck. On the boat deck, the boxes were broken open and the individual shells were passed up to men who were spaced along two narrow catwalks that hung beneath the flight deck on both sides of the boat deck.

The catwalks ran beneath the four 3-inch guns, and at each end of the catwalks was a sailor whose job was to receive a shell and push it through a 6-inch diameter hole in the flight deck. As the shell poked through the deck, a loader would grab it and load the shell into the gun. The sailor who fed shells through the deck to the number-three gun was Seaman First Class Spence.

Spence, a burly, muscular man, had been handling ammunition for nearly twenty minutes. His shirt was soaked with sweat, and he had to constantly wipe his eyes with his right forearm. Spence took a shell from the man next to him, faced aft and thrust it through the hole in the deck overhead. He stood with his arms straight above his head until he felt the round lifted, then turned, wiped his eyes, and took another shell. It seemed to be an endless exercise; take, lift, push, pause. But if Spence was getting tired he did not show it, and the urgency of his task was underscored by the growing sound of aircraft engines. The second bomb run was starting.

Lieutenant Jiro Adachi had carefully watched Lieutenant Tanabata's attack, and admired the adroit maneuver executed at the last minute by the American captain. Lieutenant Adachi, unaware of the mining effect of the two near misses, assumed that Tanabata's effort had been wasted, and resolved not to fall victim to the American's cleverness.[12]

Adachi scanned the sky around him and was pleased to see that there was still no sign of enemy fighters coming from Java, just seventy-five miles away. If they did show up he would ignore them anyway, relying on his escorting Zeros to handle them. But still, it was nice not to have enemy fighters making a nuisance of themselves during a bomb run.

The squadron leader had also noted with satisfaction that during Tanabata's run the American flak bursts had remained at a constant altitude. He correctly concluded that the Americans' guns were already firing to their maximum range and could not reach the bombers. The last observation made it obvious to Adachi that the attack would be a textbook problem.

1158-1206

Adachi formed his nine-plane squadron into three Vs of three planes each. As with Tanabata's squadron, each of his planes had a 551-pound bomb slung beneath the fuselage, and all would be dropped in one salvo. Given the plan, and Tanabata's example, Adachi knew he would get only one shot at the American ship. He did not intend to waste his shot.

As Lieutenant Adachi led his group in, the *Langley* continued to twist and turn, while her antiaircraft guns peppered the sky above her. In the radio room Radioman First Class Claud Hinds Jr. pounded out a second message, "NERK NERK V 1MZC AIR RAID RAID/WE OK."

Atop the bridge structure, Commander McConnell was again gauging the approaching aircraft trying to pick the moment of release. Though low, the antiaircraft fire was well placed and McConnell hoped it would upset the bombardiers' aim. Again the bombers' angle of elevation reached 80 degrees and the captain shouted down the voice tube, "Hard left rudder!" The *Langley* swung out from under the bombers.

At the moment the *Langley* broke left, Adachi's squadron was fast approaching the drop point—too fast in fact. As the ship dodged out of the line of attack. Adachi's speeding aircraft were caught flatfooted and overshot the turning point that would have allowed them to follow the ship around. The lead bombardier, seeing the ship move out of his sight, took his hand off the bomb release. As though making a review fly-past, the nine twin-engine bombers roared up the *Langley*'s original track and swept around for a second try.

Lieutenant Adachi, realizing that he had underestimated the American captain, led his squadron around for another run. It was obvious to the squadron leader that he would have to fly slowly to avoid overshooting the turning point when the *Langley* changed course. Because enemy flak and fighters were not a threat, Adachi throttled back, satisfied that there was nothing that would interfere with his plan.

Blanketed by the flight deck, Ensign Emmanuel could not see what was happening overhead, but he heard the engines change pitch as the bombers approached, and he could hear the *Langley*'s antiaircraft guns pounding away at the Japanese. He felt the ship twist and turn, and held his breath, expecting to hear the shriek of falling bombs and booming explosions. When he heard the engines fading away and there were no explosions, he let out a sigh of relief.

Because his 5-inch guns had no antiaircraft capability, the attack for Emmanuel and his men was a matter of waiting and hoping. Their inability to fight back put them under enormous strain, particularly when their position seemed so dangerous. "A hit back here would probably kill us all" the young ensign thought grimly. He had good reason to feel that way.

Stacked on the deck between and slightly forward of the 5-inch guns were tarpauline-covered powder bags that were part of the guns' ready ammunition. Overhead was a pyrotechnics locker and two decks below was the after 5-inch magazine. Between the guns, extending nearly to the after rail, was a large wooden structure that had been the pigeon loft during the *Langley*'s days as an aircraft carrier but now served as the executive officer's quarters. All the elements for disaster were present.

Standing near Emmanuel was the executive officer, Commander Divoll. His battle station was steering aft, from where the ship could be steered if the bridge was destroyed, or if steering was otherwise lost at the bridge. Additionally, he was responsible for supervising the damage control efforts in the after part of the ship. While Divoll was picturing in his mind the overhead events, his talker handed him the battle phone from the bridge. It was McConnell telling him to go down into the engine room and find out what was really happening there. The order probably saved his life.

Divoll descended to the main deck, entered the mess hall, and crossed quickly to the engine room ladder. Standing on the grated engine room deck he could see water swirling in the bilges just a few feet below. Water still spurted from broken connections and dripped from dozens of patches. Everything was so wet that it looked as if the engine room had been worked over with a fire hose. Divoll was listening to the engineering officer, Lieutenant N. B. "Nat" Frey, when the Japanese bombers started their third run.

1206–1214

Adachi was concentrating on the ship as his formation approached the drop point. The lieutenant, flying at minimum speed, was watching for a sign that would tell him the ship was going to turn. Suddenly, the *Langley* started to swing left. With plenty of time to react, Adachi led his bombers around with parade ground precision. The planes were now very close to the drop point.

The *Langley* was still turning left trailing a brilliant white, curving wake with Adachi dead astern cutting just a bit inside the curve. He could still see the entire ship over the nose of his bomber when he noticed a slight change in the turning radius. The *Langley* was going to turn right.

As the ship's helm went from hard left to hard right, she hesitated, straightened, and then swung over onto the new course. Adachi, prepared for the move, turned with the ship, made a minor position adjustment, and was again lined up on target. The ship's stern disappeared under the bomber's nose, and the plane lurched upward as the bomb fell away.

Torpedoman Second Class Howard Whan was sitting near the middle of the flight deck, cradling a BAR, when the bombs were released. Looking up at the bombers he saw the bombs tumble away from the aircraft and remarked that they looked like ice cubes. Not far from Whan, Fireman First Class Marvin Snyder was standing near the number-one 3-inch gun. He also saw the bombs leave the planes but thought they looked like leaflets. Nearly 300 feet away, on the signal bridge, Machinist's Mate Second Class Carl Onberg thought they looked like bombs and hit the deck.

Standing near Onberg, Commander McConnell did not see the bombs drop, but he figured that the Japanese had reached their drop point. There was another fact that he had calculated, and he shared it with Lieutenant Bailey. "If the problem is set up correctly," he told the gunnery officer, "the bombs will hit."[13]

The salvo that hurtled down toward the *Langley* was possibly the most accurate or the luckiest high-level bombing attack made on a moving ship during World War II.[14] The first bomb struck the main deck on the starboard side at the jib crane, shattered boats, started fires, and smashed a critical firemain. Shrapnel, hurled in all directions, crashed into the bridge structure and slashed through

The bridge structure as seen from the forward edge of the flight deck. The first hit exploded abaft the launch stowed in skids on the right. Commander McConnell, Lieutenant Bailey, Lieutenants Akerman and Dix, and the machine gunners were all atop the bridge structure. The radio room is the small windowed structure with the blowers on top. Carpenter Curtis, Earl Snyder, and James Childers were all hit in the passageway that passes through the bridge structure on the right. The motor whaleboat partially visible in its davits on the extreme right is the one from which the wounded were spilled into the water. (Photo courtesy of Eugene Eckstein)

the 3-inch ammunition handlers. The explosion ripped a hole in the main deck ten feet in diameter, wiped out steering control from the bridge, cut phone cables, and blew apart the boxes of 3-inch ammunition stacked outside the magazine.

Baker Third Class Wetherbee was standing above the open magazine hatch about to take a box of ammunition when the blast and heat engulfed him. A tremendous pressure drove the air from his lungs as the brilliant red flash turned instantly to a grey haze and then blackness. Wetherbee fell into the open magazine, landing heavily among the broken boxes and scattered shells.

One deck above where Wetherbee's still form lay crumbled, the passageway that ran under the starboard side of the bridge had been transformed into a bloody hell of broken bones and mangled flesh. A damage control party led by a warrant officer, Carpenter Robert Curtis, had been moving aft along the passageway toward the open main deck when the bomb exploded just eighty feet away. As though fired by a giant shotgun, jagged fragments plowed through the group. A fist-size piece of steel hit the warrant officer in the left side of his chest over the heart, and the men behind him were tossed about like dolls. Seaman Second Class Earl Snyder did a complete flip, crashed down onto the steel deck, and was landed on by Seaman First Class James Childers. Pinned down by Childers who had already passed out, and bleeding profusely from an ugly neck wound, the stunned Snyder was momentarily unaware that he had a broken arm and a serious chest injury.[15]

"They missed me. They missed me," groaned Snyder, and passed out.

In the radio room adjacent to the carpenter's shop, Claud Hinds was pounding out, "NERK NERK NQO NQO V NERK NERK BT LANGLEY LANGLEY BEING ATTACKED BY SIX-TEEN AIRCRAFT 0435 K." He was repeating the message and had just sent "ATTACKED BY" when the first bomb hit. None of the eight men in the radio room were hurt, but the transmitter was

The main deck looking aft from the forward part of the flight deck su-perstructure. The area where the two boats and equipment are stored was occasionally called the hangar deck. It was in that area that five P-40s were stowed during the crossing from Fremantle to Tjilatjap. Three-inch am-munition was brought up from the magazine through the open hatch on the right and carried aft to the poop deck. When bombs two and three hit, the area along the port side became an inferno. (Photo courtesy of Eugene Eckstein)

knocked out when the explosion severed the power lines. Chief Radioman Leland Leonard sent Seaman First Class Wilbur Naish, Seaman First Class Walter Standbury, and Seaman First Class Stanley Phillips to see about getting the ship's power restored, and then shifted over to batteries.[16]

Carl Onberg, lying on the signal bridge deck when the bomb hit, was enveloped by the deafening roar and shock wave that swept across the bridge. Metal fragments whizzed over his head, cutting down two machine gun crews and Lieutenant Bailey who was standing next to the captain. Onberg saw Lieutenant Bailey sag, a huge bloody wound in the chest, and collapse face down on the deck.

At the moment that Onberg was looking at the mutilated gunnery officer, the second and third bombs hit the port side of the elevator. Howard Whan, face down on the deck, was lifted and flipped over on his back, while around him three P-40s collapsed. Beyond destroying the three planes, the hits did surprisingly little damage on the flight deck, This may have been because the explosion was dissipated upward and out over the water, but the force that was directed downward onto the confined main deck was another matter.

The space beneath the wooden flight deck was packed with boats, equipment, and P-40s. Beneath the boats and airplanes, and behind the equipment, twenty or thirty men had taken cover when the whistling bombs had prompted several shouted warnings.

The downward force of the bomb burst erupted onto the main deck, destroyed all the boats on the port side, hurled machinery across the deck, and set the P-40s afire. Oil from smashed crankcases spilled onto the deck and fed the rapidly growing fires, as burning aircraft exploded. No one will ever know who died in the port-side inferno, though most were probably Army Air Force men who had taken cover near the aircraft.[17]

Seaman First Class Walter Kownacki was still on his feet passing 3-inch ammunition up the starboard ladder to the poop deck when suddenly everything moved as the shock wave swept down the deck. Kownacki's helmet flew off and "stuff" blew past him, ricocheting off the machinery near him. Kownacki himself was knocked flat, skidding across the deck into another man.

Just a few feet away Jim Mealley was face down under a motor whaleboat. The blast lifted him off the deck and smashed the boat he was hiding under, setting it afire. But before he was even aware of the fire directly above him, the deck convulsed again.

The fourth bomb hit the outboard edge of the stack sponson about eight feet below the edge of the flight deck. The burst rose up and out, and though partially blocked by the flight deck, it carried with it a storm of shrapnel and debris that smashed through P-40s, splinter shields, and men. Fireman First Class Henry Restorff was face down on the deck near the number-two gun when the bomb exploded fifty feet away. Nearly everyone had hit the deck, but a warrant officer, Gunner H. E. Anderson, and a loader on number-two gun, Aviation machinist's Mate Second Class Charles Soke, were standing up.

A piece of steel the size of an open hand smashed through the boiler-plate-and-cement splinter shield, hitting Soke in the back. The young sailor flopped to the deck hideously wounded and dying.[18] Gunner Anderson was sprawled on the deck, badly concussed and naked except for his steel helmet and right shoe.[19] Forty feet away Marvin Snyder and Fireman First Class Donald Brown were hugging the deck when the explosion tore the world apart around them. Airplanes slewed around, undercarriages collapsed, and P-40s burst into flame. The loader on the number-one gun was hit in the back and sank to the deck. As the man went down he asked Snyder to relieve him. The deck between the two guns was a shambles of broken, twisted, and burning fighters. Many of the men were moaning, whimpering, and crying as the bombs marched along the deck.[20]

Down in the fire room the blast had blown out the fires in all three boilers and filled the fire room with choking, eye-smarting hot gases. The *Langley* had an open fire room, which meant that the furnaces depended on a huge squirrel-cage blower built into the stack sponson to provide draft for the fires. Luckily, the explosion did not damage the blower, and once the overpowering pressure had been expended, the still-running blower started to suck the smoke and hot gases out of the fire room. The badly shaken and partially asphyxiated firemen hurriedly relit the fires.[21]

In the engine room each jolting hit had ruptured more water lines and destroyed the patches that had been put on the first holes. The water level that had remained fairly constant for the last eight minutes was again rising, and this time it rose rapidly. But the hits on deck were not the real cause of the trouble. The increased flooding had resulted from three near misses that had straddled the *Langley* just as the first three hits were made. The mining effect of the near misses on the already weakened hull was enormous, and the delicate balance between flooding and pumping had been destroyed.

On the poop deck Ensign Emmanuel was prone on the deck between the two 5-inch guns. When the first bomb struck, he had ordered all his men to get down, and then he gritted his teeth as each successive explosion rolled through the ship, coming nearer each time. The flight deck that blocked his view overhead afforded a sense of security, as did the two guns beside him and the structure behind him, But the security provided by those things was false.

The fifth bomb crashed through the wooden flight deck near the stern, and penetrated the steel poop deck with a searing flash, burning many of Ensign Emmanuel's men. Plunging down nine more feet, the bomb exploded in the starboard washroom, adjacent

Michel Emmanuel was an ensign aboard the *Langley*, in charge of the after 5-inch guns. Despite shrapnel wounds and burns he stayed at his post and directed the fire fighting on the poop deck. He is shown here in 1944 after he had transferred to naval aviation and become a "Black Cat" pilot. (Photo courtesy of Michel Emmanuel)

to the steering engine room. Immediately a fountain of flame, shrapnel, and debris erupted back through the poop deck killing, maiming, and blowing men overboard.

In that same instant the washroom bulkhead buckled outward throwing a hail of rivets across the steering engine room. Quartermaster Third Class Duane Smith died instantly, his body riddled by the deadly missiles.[22] Machinist's Mate McKinney and his four seamen assistants were knocked down, deafened, and stunned. Chief Pharmacists's mate Thomas Wetherell's left arm was broken when he was thrown against the bulkhead in the port washroom where Doctor J. F. Handley had set up the after battle dressing station.[23]

The force of the explosion ruptured the 3-inch steam line to the steering engine and jammed the rudder at 35 degrees right. Steam pouring from the broken steam line mixed with acrid smoke, blinding and choking the survivors. Overhead a fire storm swept across the ship's stern on the poop deck. Feeding on layers of paint and the executive officer's wooden quarters, the blaze soon became an inferno. Before the shocked, stunned survivors could recover, the fire ignited the powder bags stacked between the guns. An enormous explosion resulted that blew more men overboard and forced others to jump to escape the spreading fire.[24]

1214–1219

At the moment the ready ammunition blew up, Spence was facing aft, just starting to push a 3-inch shell through the hole in the deck overhead. A wall of hot air filled with birdshot-size pieces of metal slammed into the seaman, knocking him down. The man behind Spence was catapulted off the catwalk and crashed down onto the boat deck.

Spence shook the cobwebs out and fumbled for the shell that lay on the catwalk. As he stood up to push the shell through the hole, blood began running into his eyes and across his face. There was a terrible pain in his left shoulder and his right hand felt as though there was a rock buried in it. Despite the pain and growing weakness, Spence continued to stand there pushing the shell through the hole. After what seemed like an hour he shouted, "Hey! Someone take this round!" When there was no response he put the shell down and wandered off.

From left to right, the first hit was scored near the starboard jib crane, which is visible at the forward end of the flight structure. The second hit was on the port side of the elevator in about the middle of the first opening. The third hit was a little aft, near the second steel support column. The fourth hit caught the edge of the stack sponson at about the first port. The fifth hit punched through the end of the flight deck, passed between the two 5-inch guns visible on the poop deck, and exploded one deck below. (National Archives)

There was no response to Spence's shout because the number-three gun was no longer firing. The explosion of the ready ammunition had burst through the flight deck like a volcano, leaving the after portion of the flight deck littered with mangled and burning fighter planes and patches of fire that burned hotly on the wooden flight deck.

Through sheer good fortune, the number-three gun crew had suffered only one casualty. Seaman First Class Harry Mayfield had been shouting to his close friend Seaman First Class James Fecht to get down when the flight deck behind them suddenly rose up in a wall of flame. Whole airplanes were flipped over, others disintegrated or exploded, sending pieces of wing and tail spinning over the side. Out of the explosion came a chunk of steel that hit Fecht in the back, bowling him over.

Mayfield jumped to help his friend and was busy trying to stop the bleeding at about the time Spence had been poking the shell through the deck. The rest of the gun crew seemed to be dazed and unsure of what to do next. Sixty feet away Henry Restorff was helping to lay the dying loader from the number-two gun on the deck. Ensign Ditto had pulled off his white shirt and stuffed it into the hole in the boy's back, but the effort was too late; the sailor was already dead. Amid the smoke and confusion Mayfield noticed that the deck was growing hotter.

Two decks below Mayfield, Emmanuel lay bleeding on the smashed and flaming poop deck. The force of the blast had bent the rim of his "tin hat" down, jamming the helmet so tightly on his head that he had difficulty getting it off. When the helmet finally came off Emmanuel was horrified to see the decapitated body of one of the gun captains just a few feet away. Painfully getting to his feet he was further sickened at the sight of a sailor writhing on the deck with a horrible abdominal wound. The disemboweled man, suffering terribly, begged the ensign to shoot him.

It appeared to Emmanuel that everyone on the poop deck was burned or riddled with shrapnel. Feeling a sharp pain in his back, he reached around and felt a warm sticky mass. Pulling his hand away he stared at his own blood, knowing for the first time that he had been injured.

It was while Ensign Emmanuel was getting back on his feet that Commander Divoll returned to the poop deck. Divoll moved as far aft as he could before the flames and heat stopped him. Through the smoke and fire the executive officer could not see any sign of life around the 5-inch guns. The old wooden pigeon loft that had been his quarters had been reduced to a fiery framework. In that moment Divoll remembered his tailored Rice and Duval overcoat that he had paid 140 dollars for in Sydney before the war. "Damn!" he muttered, "The bastards burned up my coat."

But thoughts about his coat were quickly put out of his mind. The exec felt the ship starting to list. Divoll took another look around, concluded that everyone on the fantail had died in the inferno that was already spreading to the flight deck, and headed back toward the engine room.

In the meantime word was passed to Millard McKinney in the steering engine room that steering had been lost at the bridge. It was assumed that the steering casualty resulted from damage to the cables that ran from the steering engine to the bridge. In fact, the problem was much more serious.

McKinney disconnected the steering engine throttle from the steering cables, and attempted to move the rudder by turning the throttle wheel by hand. Nothing happened. Steam pressure had to be at least forty pounds per square inch in order for the piston to function, but because of the ruptured steam line there was not enough pressure.[25]

Machinist's Mate Second Class John "Smokey" Musser emerged from the shambles of the starboard washroom just as McKinney was disconnecting the steering throttle cables. Musser was part of a damage control party that had been in the washroom when the bomb exploded. The machinist's mate survived without a scratch, but his two companions were killed.[26] Seeing McKinney's problem, Musser called to three other sailors to lend a hand repairing the broken steam line. Grabbing a tool box Musser yelled to McKinney, "We're gonna shut off the steam. With that leak you're not getting enough pressure anyway."[27]

McKinney, in the meantime, decided to try to regain steering by attaching a larger handwheel directly to the worm gear that turned the rudder. He jumped down from the small platform near the top of the steering engine and quickly disconnected the steering engine coupling. Then he slid the large handwheel onto the shaft and bolted it in place. Turning the wheel alone would have been impossible even under normal conditions, so McKinney shouted for the three sailors to bear a hand turning the wheel. Four strong backs should have been able to do the job normally performed by the 200 horsepower steam engine. But after two or three minutes of heaving and straining the four men had been unable to budge the rudder from its hard-over-right position. McKinney concluded that the rudder was hopelessly jammed, and even if Musser was able to get the steam engine working again, the rudder could not be moved.

As the men struggled to move the rudder, wounded men were making their way through the steam and smoke to the after battle-dressing station where Doctor Handley was treating his pharmacist's compound fracture. Two mortally wounded men already lay on the floor, and ten more men with shrapnel wounds were hunched against the bulkhead or lying on the deck outside the door.[28]

In the crypto room, adjacent to the radio room, Radio Electrician Snay was trying to raise the bridge on the battle phone. The phone was dead and the warrant officer assumed that the blast, because it had been so violent, had taken out the bridge. Leaving the crypto room, Snay went into the radio room and told Leonard, "Keep things moving here. I'm going up to the bridge to see what's happening."

Outside the radio room door there was noise and confusion as men tried to get into the passageway to help the wounded and the survivors struggled to get out. The warrant officer was appalled at the apparently aimless confusion that was taking place in the passageway as he stepped out of the radio room. Taking charge, Snay sent a man down to the forward battle-dressing station to get stretcher-bearers. He then reorganized the damage control party and put survivors to work giving the wounded first aid. When things looked under control, he went up the ladder toward the bridge, fully expecting to find a similar scene up there.

At about the time that Snay was starting toward the bridge, Commander Divoll arrived in the engine room to find that the situation had become desperate. The water was now five feet deep in the bilges and rising quickly. The *Langley* was listing slightly to port, causing the water to run into the port motor pit. Lieutenant Frey had already sent a messenger to the bridge to tell the captain it was only a matter of time until he would have to shut down the motors. Even as the men talked, the water rose higher.

Overhead sixteen Japanese bombers and fifteen Zero fighters circled out of range of the *Langley*'s remaining two 3-inch guns. The Japanese airmen could see that the ship was still turning, but losing way, as fire and smoke covered two-thirds of her length. Despite the intense fires and heavy smoke, it appeared that several of the P-40s on the flight deck were undamaged, and men could be seen moving among the airplanes.

1219–1229

Lieutenant Yokoyama, leading his squadron of six Zeros, decided to go down for a closer look. Signaling to his squadron to follow, Yokoyama put his fighter into a steep dive. As the six Zeros dove toward the *Langley*, the other nine led by Lieutenant Sashio Maki began to climb and head south. Closing on the ship, Yokoyama noted that she was listing, and saw an enormous blackened hole, surrounded by broken and burning aircraft, near the after end of the flight deck. The hole seemed to be filled with fire, and men were jumping off the stern. Forward of the hole were a few undamaged planes, then more smashed and burning fighters followed by a small group of apparently whole aircraft. On the forward part of the flight deck were more burning P-40s.

Yokoyama saw men hit the deck as he bore in, pumping 20-millimeter cannon fire into the undamaged fighters. The explosive shells stitched a path of destruction along the deck, setting more P-40s afire. Yokoyama saw tiny flashes of machine gun fire sparkling along the top of the bridge and red tracers streaked toward him. Lifting the Zero's nose up slightly, he fired a burst of cannon fire into the bridge and then pulled up steeply, climbing away from the burning ship.

Right behind the squadron leader came Yokoyama's wingman, chewing up the flight deck and damaging more fighters. The stationary planes shuddered as the heavy cannon fire drummed along their fuselages and wings, tearing off huge pieces of metal and starting fires. Five more planes were hit and one exploded, destroying the planes around it. The wingman also saw the twinkling lights on the signal bridge and recognized them as machine gun fire. Adjusting his fire to the new target, he hosed the bridge structure with a long burst as he pulled up and climbed away.

When Yokoyama started his strafing run, the gun crews had just started to carry the seriously wounded men below. At the sound of the approaching Zeros' howling engines, everyone fell to the deck. Howard Whan saw the fighters coming in very low from astern and could even make out the pilot's head as the first plane drew closer. Frantically, Whan fumbled with his BAR in a desperate effort not to miss the chance of a lifetime.

"God damn! That SOB's gonna be right in my lap!" said the torpedoman aloud to himself. As Yokoyama thundered over, almost at deck level, Whan sprayed the air with .30-caliber bullets, while cursing the fact that he had never had any training with the weapon.

On the bridge, the wounded machine gunners' places had been taken over by Commander McConnell and the two Army pilots. McConnell was blazing away at the strafers from the port bridge wing, while Akerman and Dix hammered away from the starboard wing. There was a measure of grim humor in the situation. The two pilots had been trained for the day when they would engage an enemy pilot in combat, and the weapon they would use was the Browning .50-caliber machine gun. Now the day had come and all the elements were present, but the enemy pilot was the only one who had an airplane.

As Yokoyama beat up the flight deck, both machine guns reached out for the plane with a steady stream of bullets and tracers. Joining the chattering machine guns was Carl Onberg's BAR. The seaman, unlike Whan, was fully familiar with the automatic rifle and had been firing since the Zero was first spotted diving at the ship. By the time both planes had passed over, Onberg had used up his entire supply of ammunition.

The machine guns were also eating up ammunition. Gerald Dix was sighting through the ring sight and gripping the yoke handles tightly to control the shaking gun. Akerman was reaching for the nearly empty ammunition drum, preparing to remove it and slap in a full one, when one of the last rounds fired by the strafers struck the machine gun. The 20-millimeter shell exploded in a fiery flash that tore the gun apart and blew broken pieces back into Dix's face. A large chunk of steel hit the airman on the jaw shattering the bone. Akerman, reaching for the empty ammunition drum, was slashed across the back of the left hand by a steel sliver that severed the tendons.

As the Zeros thundered over the bridge and started to climb they were pursued by an angry hail of bullets from the three remaining guns. The fighters were quickly out of range and the guns stopped firing. Dix was sitting on the deck, dazed and bleeding heavily from the mouth, Akerman kneeling beside him. A pharmacist's mate was hurriedly tending the badly wounded Lieutenant Bailey while stretcher-bearers picked up the other wounded. Charles Snay had just stepped onto the signal bridge and was talking to Commander McConnell, telling him that most of the ship's communications system had been knocked out. The news worried McConnell, who could imagine the problems that were occurring throughout his stricken ship. Without communications, he would have to rely on the painfully slow method of using messengers.

"Get a message out that we have been attacked by land-based bombers. Stress land-based," he told Snay.[29] Then he sent his talker to the flight deck with orders for Yeoman Kennedy to report to the bridge. With the ship's communications system out, the talkers would be better employed as runners. Suddenly there was a shouted warning, "Here they come again!"

The Zeros were coming in from the bow in a rough diamond-shaped formation that had two planes on the bottom, one at each side, and two at the top. The pattern slanted back, from bottom to top, so that the bottom pair of Zeros were well ahead of the two mid-level planes, which in turn were well ahead of the top pair. It was an unusual formation that allowed only the two bottom planes to make an effective strafing run. In fact only one pilot, probably Yokoyama, made a determined effort to strafe the ship on the second pass.[30]

As the planes swept across the water toward the ship, Ensign Asdell and his gunners scrambled for cover behind their 5-inch guns and the huge anchor windlass that was mounted in the middle of the deck. Charles Snay darted for a ladder as Commander McConnell grabbed the yoke handle on a .50-caliber machine gun and swung the barrell toward the advancing planes.

Bullets raked the forecastle and the face of the bridge structure, splintering the teak deck and smashing windows. Caught on the exposed ladder, Snay dove head first, landing painfully at the base of the ladder. As he crashed on the deck, a BAR-man a few feet away was hit hard and went down. Bullets splattered against the steel above Snay's head, pelting his neck and shoulders with fragments.

At the base of the bridge structure, on the starboard side, were Coxswain John Bartuck and several seamen. They had miraculously survived the bomb hits without a scratch, but Bartuck did not think their luck would hold any longer as Yokoyama's Zero bore in. The only shelter appeared to be under the flight deck about seventy feet away. The sailors were sprinting across the open main deck when Yokoyama passed over. Cannon and machine gun rounds exploded and ricocheted around them as they ran. The man in front of Bartuck suddenly went down, arms and legs flailing. Behind him three more sailors were hit. Long after the fighter had passed, John Bartuck reached the safety of the flight deck.

Also caught on the open main deck was John Kennedy. After reporting to the captain, Kennedy had been sent down to the main deck to fight fires that were burning in the boats. When sending the young yeoman off, McConnell had said, "Go see about putting the fires out in those boats, we may need them."[31]

Kennedy was wielding a CO_2 bottle when the first fighter dove at the ship. He could hear the plane's engine getting louder and then suddenly there was a hellish din around and above him as cannon and machine gun fire splattered the steel deck. Kennedy tossed the fire extinguisher into the burning boat and dove onto the narrow well deck as Yokoyama's Zero thundered over.

The six Zeros passed quickly over the *Langley* and climbed away. As the roar of their engines faded, the chattering machine gun fire from the ship also died away. The danger passed, men came out from under cover, and from here and there came shouts for stretcher-bearers. The strafing run had been at best a half-hearted attempt, and there had been little new damage and only a few casualties.

As the fighters climbed they circled, and Commander McConnell warned the men around him to be ready for another run. But to his relief, instead of coming back the Zeros formed up with the bombers and turned toward home. To the south, McConnell saw what looked like the other fighter squadron attacking a large flying boat. Suddenly there was a cloud of black smoke and McConnell saw a large object, trailing smoke, follow a slanted path to the sea. The captain's stomach tightened as the fighters reformed and wheeled around as if to return to the *Langley*. But instead they continued on around and headed off to the east; the attack was over.[32]

The *Langley* was now listing and turning slowly into the wind, clouds of oily smoke pouring from several raging fires. The flight deck was a shambles of broken, twisted, and burning aircraft. The old aircraft elevator was oddly askew and the main deck below it looked like a smoking junkyard. McConnell could only guess at the intensity of the fires burning out of control beneath the flight deck, but he knew they were bad. In some places they were starting to burn through the flight deck.

The captain looked at his watch and noted that just thirty-nine minutes had passed since the enemy planes had been sighted. As he turned to meet a messenger he noticed something else—the ship was losing way.[33]

CHAPTER 5

Damage Control

The messenger that McConnell turned to meet was from the engine room, and he brought Frey's warning that the motors would have to be shut down. But that disheartening report was already superseded by the report that had not yet reached the bridge—the motors had already been shut down. As he stood listening to the messenger, Commander McConnell probably suspected the worst had already happened. He had felt his ship losing way even before the messenger had arrived, and now the *Langley* was nearly dead in the water.

Six minutes after the last Zero had disappeared a wry message crackled from the tender's antenna that reflected the captain's feelings, "MOMMA SAID THERE WOULD BE DAYS LIKE THIS. . . SHE MUST HAVE KNOWN."[1]

In the engine room the motors were dead, the drive shafts motionless as the water swirled through the bilges and poured into the motor pits. Lieutenant Frey had sent Machinist Butts off on one last attempt to locate the flooding source, while the Koepsell brothers, drenched to the skin, were busy applying patches to new leaks and replacing the original patches that had been blown off. It was a hopelss task, and the water continued to rise at an alarming rate. Already the engine room deck plates were nearly awash.

In the fire rooms the situation looked less grim than it really was. The deck plates in the fire rooms were slightly higher than in the engine room, and though the firemen could see the water through the grates, their compartment was dry. The only evidence of just how serious the situation was came from the increasing list and the hiss of steam escaping through the "popped" safety valves.

Commander Divoll entered the engine room for the third time just as Butts returned from his inspection tour. The warrant officer told Frey and Divoll that he had been unable to locate the exact source of the flooding. "It seems to be coming from all over," he told them.[2]

His inability to locate the exact source of the flooding was understandable—there was no exact source. The two near misses from the first salvo and the three from the second had opened riveted seams from about the engine room to the bow along the port side. The *Langley*, having been designed originally as a coal collier, had more in common with a bulk cargo carrier than with a fully compartmented warship. Adding to the problem was that water pouring from broken firemains was flooding compartments above the waterline and adding to the top weight.[3]

As the men talked the list increased, causing the water to lap at the bottom of the port motor. Even on the high side the water was over three feet deep in the motor pit, and the overworked bilge pumps were falling steadily behind. Under the circumstances the motors were finished, victims of uncontrollable flooding. But as the flooding continued, the concern that had centered on keeping the motors dry was replaced by the threat of capsizing.[4]

Even under the best conditions, the *Langley* was not a particularly stable ship. The top weight created by her heavy flight deck had been made greater by the addition of the four 3-inch guns, and had increased dramatically when the P-40s had been put aboard. As the ship listed, the forces trying to pull her over on her side increased while her already diminished natural righting forces were further decreased. Commander Divoll figured that the list, already approaching 10 degrees, would become critical when it reached 40 degrees. It was obvious to Divoll that unless something could be done to stop or slow the list, it would be simply a matter of time until she rolled over. How much time, he could not say, but he and Lieutenant Frey did not think it would be too long. The solution, of course, was to get the ship back on an even keel, and this now became the focus of their efforts. Telling Lieutenant Frey to "keep at it," Divoll headed toward the bridge to report the situation to the captain, and to recommend counter-flooding.

While Divoll was in the engine room, Ensign Emmanuel was again trying to get on his feet, assisted by Boatswain's Mate Second Class Jesse Sellers. It was a painful effort. In addition to burns, and fragments in his back, Emmanuel had also been hit in the left knee. Burned and bloody, the two men stumbled through the thick, acrid smoke until they found a fire hose. While Sellers stood by the valve, Emmanuel dragged the hose across the deck toward the fire.[5]

The ensign could see several wounded men lying on the deck and others trying to crawl away from the fire. Through the smoke he could see forms leaping from the stern to escape the inferno. There was nothing he could do for the wounded at that moment. His biggest concern was to knock the fire down before it ignited the pyrotechnics locker overhead or spread downward to the 5-inch magazine. Yelling to Sellers to turn on the water, be braced himself to take the surge when the line was charged. Nothing happened—there was no water.

On the poop deck the roar of the fire drowned out all other noise as Ensign Emmanuel retreated from the heat and rejoined Sellers. At this moment Commander Divoll joined the pair, having interrupted his trip to the bridge to assess the situation at Emmanuel's station.

Shouting to make himself heard, Emmanuel told the exec about the lack of water and Sellers warned of the danger to the 5-inch magazine. Divoll, alarmed, tried to contact the bridge on the battle phone, but the line was dead. Replacing the phone, he hurried toward the bridge.[6]

Shortly after Divoll left, Emmanuel hobbled forward to find the damage control officer, Lieutenant Commander Donovan. He found the harried Donovan on the main deck near the burning fighter planes. The ensign told him there was no water aft, and a major fire was spreading rapidly. The first lieutenant told Emmanuel that the hits had shattered most of the cast iron firemains and that he was doing his best to restore water. He suggested that as a stop-gap measure Emmanuel should have his people round up all the CO_2 bottles they could find and start with them.

Running aft as fast as he could on his injured knee, the ensign was appalled to see that the fire was already moving forward into the wooden structure on the boat deck, and was spreading along the bottom of the flight deck. Arriving at the after steering station, Emmanuel shouted orders to collect all the CO_2 bottles the men could find.[7]

In the meantime, the resourceful Boatswain Sellers had also run forward looking for a water source. He located a working firemain on the port main deck and started dragging the fire hose that was attached to it back along the main deck toward the poop deck, shouting to other men to lend a hand. As they struggled aft with the fire hose, Sellers continued to shout orders, directing men to bring more hose sections. Shortly after Ensign Emmanuel had returned to the fire, a sweating, puffing Sellers dragged the first working fire hose onto the fire line.[8]

As Divoll made his way forward through the confusion of men running to help fight the numerous fires burning along the main deck, Thomas Spence was staggering aft along the catwalk beneath the flight deck. Partially blinded by blood running from his lacerated forehead, the seaman groped for a ladder that would take him down to the boat deck.

Finding the ladder, Spence started down and almost fell when he tried to use his injured right hand to grasp a rung. Reaching the bottom of the ladder, he started forward and had gone only a short distance when he saw a man painfully dragging himself along the deck. Despite his own wounds, Spence wiped the blood from his eyes and went to the man's aid. He found that the wounded sailor was the ammunition passer who had been blown off the catwalk when the last bomb exploded.

Spence reassured the sailor while he determined how badly hurt he was. On one buttock was a bloody wound from which a fist-size chunk of meat had been gouged. Spence did not have anything with which to bandage the wound or to stop the bleeding, and it was obvious that he had to get the man to a dressing station as quickly as possible. Helping the man up and supporting him, they hobbled off toward Doctor Handley's after battle-dressing station.

The situation in the smoke-filled after battle-dressing station was very bad, and Doctor Handley already had more to do than he could handle. Three seriously wounded men had already died and ten more cases, three serious, needed his immediate attention. The doctor knew that the heat and smoke would soon make the washroom unusable, and he resolved to move to a new location as soon as possible.[9]

The ship's dentist, Doctor C. W. Holly, and the injured Chief Pharmacist's Mate Wetherell were doing what they could to help when Spence and the wounded sailor lurched into the battle-dressing station. It quickly became obvious that Spence, though bloody, was not badly injured. Doctor Holly jabbed him with a syringe of morphine and turned to the more seriously wounded sailor.

As the drug began to take effect, Spence left the dressing station and climbed back to the poop deck. The scene that confronted him there was distorted by shock and morphine, and the burly seaman found himself in an unreal world of smoke and fire. He wanted to help fight the fire, but, as in a nightmare, his efforts were ineffective.

Forward, on the second deck, Doctor Robert Blackwell was receiving casualties in the sick bay. Carpenter Curtis was already dead and Lieutenant Bailey was in bad shape. Eight more men were brought in, two seriously wounded. By now, however, the list was becoming so pronounced that anything other than first aid was practically impossible. The doctor could do little more than control bleeding, apply dressings, and administer morphine.[10]

One deck above the sick bay, in the radio room, the five radiomen and two seamen had just gotten their first report on the ship's condition. Radioman Second Class Warnes had been called out of his station in radio repair and had been sent off on another assignment. When he returned to the radio room he reported that the ship had been hit on the forecastle, the well deck, and the flight deck. He described damage to the aircraft and reported that there were "gas fumes on the well deck."[11] Warnes's report was second hand and not entirely accurate, but it convinced the radio room crew that the ship was in serious trouble, and the radio operators put the information out on all four frequencies. At 1242 Radioman First Class Hinds added, "DECIDED LIST."

When the message went out, Divoll and McConnell were stand-

Radioman First Class David Jones aboard the USS *Nevada* before transferring to the *Langley*. (Photo courtesy of David Jones)

ing on the signal bridge discussing the situation. The two officers were faced with two major problems. On one hand, the fires had to be brought under control because the ship, with 50,000 gallons of aviation fuel stored in tanks below, was essentially a flaming bomb primed to explode. The fact that the 5-inch magazine was directly under the inferno on the poop deck doubled the danger. On the other hand, fighting fires would be of little importance if the *Langley* rolled over; and the list was steadily increasing. McConnell pretty well summed up the situation when he told Divoll, "We're in a hell of a fix."[12]

The first task was to slow the list, and if possible get the ship back on an even keel, and McConnell ordered counterflooding. He hoped that when the list was reduced and the fires were under control, there might be some hope of pumping out enough water that at least the starboard motor could be restarted. As an additional step toward reducing the list, the captain ordered Divoll to push as many P-40s as possible off the flight deck, on the correct assumption that the weight of the aircraft, about ninety tons, was reducing the ship's stability to a dangerous degree.[13]

McConnell told his executive officer that if those steps were successful and if one or both of the motors could be restarted, he intended to make for the coast of Java, and if necessary, beach the ship. He reasoned that in her present condition the *Langley* could not negotiate the narrow, twisting channel into Tjilatjap, and there was no hope of reaching Australia. Looking at the smoking, twisted rubble on the flight deck, it was obvious that he could not carry out his original mission.[14]

As Divoll hurried away to carry out the captain's orders, McConnell told the navigator to lay a course to Tjilatjap. The commander was unaware that even if Divoll was able to correct the list and the fires could be brought under control, his ship could not proceed to Java because the rudder was still jammed hard over. At that time the captain believed that steering had been regained at the bridge.[15] His ignorance of the truth was due to the lack of communications.

The situation in which McConnell found himself was not unusual aboard the *Langley* at that time. The loss of the ship's communications system had isolated individuals and groups of men from one another and from the captain. Though there was no panic, there was a fair amount of aimless wandering and a lot of confusion.

As a result, officers and petty officers in charge at any location could only muster the men who were immediately available. Isolated and without direct communications to the bridge, those leaders did their best with what they had, often unaware that additional, organized help was close at hand. The result was an overall lack of coordination of efforts. Some jobs were done with more men than were needed while others were completely ignored.[16]

One group that remained inactive as a result of being isolated was a damage control party stationed in the mess hall on the main deck. Despite the fact that this group of six men was in a position to assist fighting fire on the poop deck, just above them, or on the main deck just forward of them, they were never called out.

Apparently, they were aware that something pretty bad had happened in the after part of the ship and wondered aloud if they should go find out just how bad things were. While they talked, wounded men came into the mess hall, and several people, including the executive officer, passed through on various errands. They remained where they were, however, because the senior man correctly pointed out that their duty was to remain available when needed. To go charging off in all directions would defeat the purpose of their assignment. And so they waited for a call that never came.[17]

Above the mess hall, Ensign Martin was similarly isolated in the wardroom. But his involvement in the rapidly unfolding events came with gruesome suddenness. As he sat alone at a table, he heard someone excitedly shouting, "Fire aft! Fire aft!" The young Supply Corps ensign jumped to his feet and started for the door. Just then the door opened and a badly wounded sailor flopped into the wardroom and tried to drag himself across the floor.

Martin stared, horrified, at the moaning man who was clawing his way across the deck. The seaman's right hip had been blown away. Reacting without being fully aware of what he was doing, the officer crossed the room, rolled the sailor onto his good side, and stuffed a shirt into the wound to slow the bleeding. After making the man as comfortable as possible, Martin left to find the stretcher-bearers.

Ensign Martin ran aft and into the smoke-filled steering engine room arriving at the after battle-dressing station just as the two doctors were starting their move to a new location. Martin told Doctor Handly about the sailor in the wardroom, and as luck would have it that was where the doctors were going.

After the patients had been moved out, Millard McKinney found himself alone in the steering engine room. He had tried every way he knew to free the rudder, but the job was too big for one man. Looking carefully at the steering gear, he concluded that the explosion must have bent the rudder post somewhere below the main deck. Since he could not do any more with the rudder, he decided he would be more useful fighting the fire one deck above him.

Despite the fact that he had survived the blast in an enclosed space, McKinney was not prepared for the scene that confronted him on the poop deck. The entire stern seemed to be on fire. Smoke, hot gases, and flame were pouring through a huge hole in the flight deck. Through the flames and smoke he saw figures leaping from the stern to escape the fire.

Dashing along the port rail, McKinney joined the growing group that Ensign Emmanuel was directing. Some men had large CO_2 bottles, the pressurized contents of which they were spraying on the fire. Two or three fire hoses were in operation and more were being connected to large foam hoppers. McKinney joined the latter group and was soon pouring 5-gallon cans of CO_2 foam mix into the wheeled hoppers. Mixed with water from Sellers's emergency firemain, the chemical was sucked through a fire hose and sprayed as thick foam on the fire.

On the main deck there was little fire along the starboard side though there was ample evidence of the violence that resulted from the second and third hits. Damaged P-40s, rivers of oil from broken crankcases, and boats that had been reduced to kindling littered the deck. On the port side a hot fire consumed two of the fighters and was spreading to a third. Water gushing from shattered firemains on the starboard side sloshed in the well deck and flowed across the canted main deck.

But there were already signs that the situation might be improving. Water had been restored forward, lines were being run aft along the main deck and up to the flight deck, and the ship's electrical power had been fully restored at 1230.[18] It appeared that damage control was on the way toward bringing the fires under control, and that was at least half the battle. If the other half went as well, there was still some hope of saving the ship.

Splashing his way aft along the starboard well deck through the wrecked boats and planes, John Bartuck spotted several wounded men sprawled beneath the planes. Most of them were covered with oil and appeared from their uniforms to be Army Air Force men. But just ahead he recognized his friend Gunner's Mate First Class Dwight Jones crumpled on the deck. Kneeling, Bartuck examined the unconscious Jones for visible injuries, but found none and assumed that he was a concussion victim. After dragging his friend to a fairly clear place on the deck, Bartuck went aft to find help.

His search led him to the foam and ash-slickened poop deck where he tripped over fire hoses and skirted groups of shouting men working near the fire. Stopping two stretchers-bearers coming along the deck, Bartuck told them about Jones and then moved aft to lend a hand fighting fire. While helping a group of men with a foam hopper, he saw a macabre scene that was permanently branded in his mind. On one side of the fiery, crumbling executive officer's quarters was the perfect imprint of a man who had been blown through the wall.

Ensign Emmanuel now had water, CO_2 foam, and increasing manpower with which to fight the blaze on the poop deck. His major concern was to keep the fire away from the pyrotechnics locker overhead, and to prevent the fire from spreading downward. Unknown to the ensign, the pyrotechnics locker was empty, the contents having been stuck below several days earlier.[19]

But now a new threat appeared. Either fire from the five P-40s parked on the main deck had spread downward, or smoldering fires that had been started below decks by the first bomb hit had suddenly come to life. At 1240 a fire was reported in the 3-inch magazine.[20]

In the magazine, Frank Wetherbee was slowly regaining consciousness. As he came to, he experienced a tremendous pressure in his ears and saw "little streaks of green lightning jumping all over the place." The magazine was dark and filled with smoke, but there was light coming through a ten-foot hole in the overhead. Wetherbee got slowly to his feet, stumbling over the broken ammunition boxes and loose 3-inch rounds scattered on the deck. From somewhere he could hear a hissing noise, like high-pressure steam escaping. There was no one else in the magazine that he could see, but he did hear someone shouting to clear the area because the magazine was to be flooded immediately. Still groggy, the huge baker lurched to a ladder, climbed out of the magazine, and made his way to the main deck.

The fresh air helped to clear the fog and he became aware of the destruction around him. Fighter planes were scattered helter-skelter, and there was oil everywhere. Near one of the planes he saw an oil-covered Army man "groveling around." Wetherbee helped the airman up, and was able to walk the unsteady man to the poop deck. During their trip aft, Wetherbee tried to see if the man had any visible injuries, but he was so coated with oil that the attempt was futile.

There were several fires burning beneath the flight deck, and more were starting to flare up along the port side. Several groups

of men were already fighting the fires and more were being organized. Wetherbee and the injured airman kept to the starboard
side and soon passed Wetherbee's abandon-ship station about amidships. The sailor noted that where there had been a motor launch,
there were now only charred remains.

After gaining the poop deck, they ran into a group of Army
men, and Wetherbee let go of his charge, who staggered forward
two or three steps and collapsed. The baker made a hurried, but
closer, examination of the injured man and this time he found a
chunk of steel in the back of his skull. With the aid of an airman,
Wetherbee carried the unconscious man to the wardroom.

While Wetherbee was helping the airman aft, tons of seawater
poured into the 3-inch magazine. At the same time Lieutenant Frey
started pumping fuel oil from the port tanks into the starboard
tanks. Because the ship was down by the bow the first transfer was
made from the forward port tank to the after starboard tank. The
initial effort was ineffective and Frey ordered all tanks along the
port side progressively pumped out, filling those along the starboard side.[21] But the *Langley*'s hull was too badly damaged and the
weight of the water that entered was greater than the weight of
the transferred fuel. Adding to the problem was the water that was
now filling the 3-inch magazine plus the water that cascaded down
from the broken firemains. About the best that had been achieved
by Frey's efforts was to have momentarily slowed the list.

While the pumping was in progress, Commander Divoll was
organizing the second part of the plan to bring the ship back on
an even keel. As he was discussing the plan with Ensign Ditto, Divoll
looked around the littered flight deck and saw several planes on
fire and patches of fire burning through the wooden flight deck.
Two of the 3-inch guns were still manned but with reduced crews.
The wounded had been taken below, and the remainder of Ditto's
gunners were fighting fire abaft the guns with hoses that snaked
up from the main deck.

It was apparent to the two officers that relieving the tender of
her top weight was not going to be an easy matter. Many of the
burning planes were too hot to get near, and exploding .50-caliber
ammunition was an added hazard. There were several relatively
undamaged planes on the deck. Those planes were not burning

and their landing gear was intact, tires still inflated. It would have been an easy matter to push those planes over the side had they been in the right place.

In order to achieve the maximum effect from pushing the fighters overboard, they would have to be removed from the port side. Unfortunately, that is where the most heavily damaged planes were, and pushing them over the side would be no easy matter. The landing gear had collapsed on most of them, their backs were broken, and wings sagged from the roots. A P-40E, empty, weighed about 6,400 pounds.[22] Give or take a few hundred pounds for added combat equipment such as guns and radios, or missing parts such as chunks of wings and tails, each plane represented at least three and one-third tons of deadweight. The planes would be hard to move, but the 10-degree list would help a little.

It would take about twenty-five sailors and airmen to do the job. To get that number, Divoll had to strip the gun crews. This was not as drastic as it sounds. If the Japanese returned, there would be enough men readily available to man at least two, or possibly three, of the guns. But without ammunition—there were no ammunition passers, and the 3-inch magazine was flooded—manning the guns would have been nothing more than a gesture anyway.

Calling the men together, Divoll explained what was to be done. The work would start with the least-damaged planes along the port side. Sweating, straining, and heaving, the sailors and airmen pushed and humped the first P-40 across the slopping deck and over the edge. The work was slow and hard, and as the first fighter slowly tumbled over the edge, the panting laborers gave a cheer.

James Mealley was fighting fire on the main deck just below the forward edge of the flight deck. A heavy layer of foam covered the deck, which—combined with the sloping deck—made it very hard to move about. Slipping and sliding, Mealley and his mates struggled forward along the port rail. Ahead of him, Mealley could see the fire-blackened remains of the number-two motor launch. The sight disappointed the young seaman who, as the boat's coxswain, had taken great pride in her appearance. He also saw that the

Seaman First Class James Mealley (far right) was in the 3-inch ammunition party when the second and third bombs hit. He was saved by the 18-inch rise of the old coal bunker hatch coaming. (Photo courtesy James Mealley)

boat's brass, horseshoe-shaped taffrail had been blown off and had made a perfect "ringer" around the foremast at the yardarm.

Mealley's thoughts were frighteningly interrupted when the first P-40 came tumbling from the flight deck and crashed into the water alongside. At first Mealley thought the ship was rolling over and that the lose hulks were sliding off the flight deck. As quickly as the thought had come, he discounted it when he realized that the list was still only about 10 degrees.

The sound of falling aircraft also alarmed Lester Bates, whose damage control party was also fighting fires under the flight deck. Aided by several Army men, the sailors were concentrating on knocking down the fires that were consuming the boats stored along the port side. It was a hot and dangerous task complicated by dense, eye-smarting smoke and the presence of another fire burning overhead along the bottom of the flight deck. Machinist's Mate First

Class Richard Shanley, one of the men fighting the fires, later described the scene:

> There were fires all over the place beneath the flight deck, with a lot of flame and smoke. The entire superstructure—the supports and framework for the flight deck—was burning due to so many coats of paint.[23]

Feeding on those layers of paint, the overhead fire became a flaming storm that rained burning paint and hot metal down on the men below.

More men were joining the fire-fighting crew, and several were detailed to fight the overhead fire—the battle becoming three dimensional as hoses were hauled up to the catwalks. Hundreds of gallons of seawater quickly cooled the fire, replacing the rain of hot paint and metal with one of wet ash and soot.

Another airplane rolled off the flight deck, doing a quarter cartwheel as it plunged into the sea. A portion of the tail smashed a burning boat as the fighter struck the water, scattering the pieces and putting out the fire. As the *Langley*'s list continued to increase, loose equipment and wreckage began sliding across the oil-, water-, and foam-covered decks. With increasing frequency heavy items began spilling from the ship's low side.

Word was now passed that electricians were needed in the gyro room. Bates was only too happy to get away from the acrid fumes and grime on the main deck and immediately answered the call. Though the ship was listing badly, Bates had little trouble negotiating the lower passages. As he worked his way lower in the ship, he saw more and more evidence of flooding.

The gyro room was a separate compartment set inside a larger compartment. In fact, the larger compartment had once been a coal bunker. The water in the surrounding hold was already a foot and a half deep, but had not started to flow over the hatch coamings into the gyro room.

Inside the gyro room he found more evidence of the violent pounding those near misses had given the old tender. Rivets blown from the bulkhead had streaked across the compartment causing terrible damage. Personal lockers were riddled with holes, and the electrical control panels were smashed. It did not take long for Bates to determine that the *Langley*'s gyros could not be repaired.

While Lester Bates was inside the gyro room, Ensign Martin was walking aft along the poop deck with an axe in his hand, intending to help fight fire. Exactly what he intended to do with the axe is not clear, but at the time it seemed to him to be a useful tool. The ensign arrived at the fire at about the time that Ensign Emmanuel and his sweating sailors were bringing the fire under control. It was no longer spreading and in a large area the fire had been beaten down. There was still plenty of fire overhead on the flight deck and along the starbord rail, but the situation was definitely improving. Seeing that he was not needed, Ensign Martin handed his axe to a seaman and went below to the supply office, located on the second deck near the 3-inch magazine.

Commander McConnell was experiencing a growing sense of frustration at about the time that Martin was descending to the supply office. Situation reports were sketchy and took a long time to reach him. The last reports had been glum, describing rising water in the engine room, a fire in the 3-inch magazine, and several out-of-control fires under the flight deck. He now had a report that the gyro was damaged beyond repair, and he estimated the list had reached 15 degrees. Obviously the counterflooding measure had been ineffective, and Divoll's effort to reduce the ship's top weight was similarly so. The only bright spot was the fact that most of the fires that burned along two-thirds of the ship's length were being put out or brought under control.

Nearly 500 feet aft and two decks lower, Frank Wetherbee was just entering the bake shop. When Wetherbee's massive form entered, his friends Riley and McLean jumped up to greet him. Suddenly William Boone, a cook, rushed over and dumped a bucket of water down Frank's neck and back. Wetherbee, in no mood for pranks, turned angrily on the much smaller Boone. Riley and McLean leaped on their friend to restrain him from punching poor Boone in the nose. Bewildered and still angry, Wetherbee sat down as Riley pulled off his kapok life jacket. It was then that Wetherbee understood Boone's action. Lodged in the back of his now-smoldering life jacket was a hot shell fragment. Mollified, the baker carefully rolled the piece of jagged metal in his hankerchief and stuffed in into his pocket. A few moments later another friend entered the bake shop.

The newcomer was Chief Commissary Steward George Vano, who staggered in with a bloody head wound. Vano looked awful. His hair was caked with blood, and the shoulders and back of his shirt were soaked through to the skin. Quickly Riley and Mclean led him to a chair while Wetherbee grabbed the bake shop's first aid kit. Luckily, Vano's wound was less serious than it had first appeared, and by the time Wetherbee had bandaged him, Vano was feeling much better.

One deck higher, Ensign Emmanuel was starting to feel the effects of his wounds. He was bleeding more heavily and his knees were shaky as he moved from point to point directing the fire fighting on the poop deck. The fire was nearly under control, though there were still some hot spots, and the flight deck around the bomb hole was now fully involved. Leaving Sellers in charge, the wounded ensign limped to the wardroom, hoping to have his wounds looked at. But when he stepped inside, he saw that Doctor Handley, assisted by the ship's dentist, Doctor Holly, already had more work than they could handle. Emmanuel turned around and went back to fighting fire.

The ship had developed a severe list by the time Ensign Martin reached the supply office. Water swirled in the hold below; boxes, paper supplies, and unidentifiable small items floated like survivors of a shipwreck. On the still-dry supply office floor were scattered the carefully kept supply, pay, and personnel records, which Martin hurriedly gathered up and put in a bag.

On the bridge, Commander McConnell had just received the dismal report from the engine room that the fire room bilges were awash and there were four feet of water in both motor pits. The report was already seven to eight minutes old and McConnell could tell that things had not improved since then.

He watched as Divoll's work party shoved the third P-40 off the flight deck. The battered fighter shed its left wing as the plane hung on the edge. Grunting and groaning the men lifted the plane's tail, shoving it to the left to dislodge the plane from its precarious perch. Finally gravity took over and the plane slid sideways off the deck, rolling over on its back before it hit the water.

By this time McConnell realized that efforts to reduce the ship's top weight were as ineffective as counterflooding had been. The list was now 15 degrees and increasing. On the bright side, there were reports that the fires were nearly under control, but considering all the other factors the captain was not optimistic. At about 1300 he told Yeoman Kennedy to pass the word to prepare to abandon ship.[24]

McConnell had not yet given up the fight to save his ship and only wanted the serviceable boats and life rafts made ready for lowering. As the word was passed, however, the order was either improperly repeated or misunderstood, and many men began jumping from the ship. As the early jumpers hit the water, the *Edsall* moved in and began fishing them out.

When the word to prepare to abandon ship reached Doctor Blackwell, he immediately started moving the seriously wounded men up to the main deck.[25] Emerging from the base of the bridge structure, the doctor was appalled at the extent of the damage and was surprised that he had not seen more wounded men. The stretcher cases were laid out on the starboard deck near the number-one motor whaleboat. Miraculously, that boat had come through the attack undamaged, while everything around it had taken a terrible beating. Doctor Blackwell moved among his patients making sure that each one had a life jacket and that none of the dressings had come loose during the move.

The stretcher cases from Doctor Handley's after battle-dressing station were soon brought forward and laid out on the main deck. The boat at their abandon-ship station had been destroyed, and it was a relief to Doctor Handley to learn that the number-one motor whaleboat was still intact. Some of the ambulatory wounded from both dressing stations were sitting among the stretcher cases, but others had left to fend for themselves, such as Earl Snyder.

Snyder had been taken below to Doctor Blackwell along with Curtis and Childers, one near death and the other unconscious. The doctor, unable to help Curtis, had treated Childers first and then turned to Snyder. At that time the ship's list was only slight, and Blackwell had been able to put a cast on Snyder that covered his broken arm and encased his upper body.

Later, when the wounded were moved to the main deck, Snyder—though hazy from morphine—was ambulatory. Though drugged and in shock, he realized that the order to abandon ship would soon be given, and he did not want to go over the side, even in a boat, wearing the heavy cast. His cast was apparently so bulky that the medics had been unable to fit a life jacket over it. As a result, Snyder considered the cast a liability, and he left the group to find some way to break off the plaster. Leaving the wounded may have saved his life.

About ten minutes after his unsuccessful attempt to have his wounds looked at, Ensign Emmanuel received word to prepare to abandon ship. He and his men had been fighting fire for nearly fifty minutes. The ensign was red-eyed, exhausted, and weak from loss of blood. His men were in the same shape and some had minor wounds. The fire, though still burning, had been knocked down and was not spreading. At 1310 Emmanuel released the men from their fire-fighting duties, telling them to get ready to leave the ship.

In the supply office Ensign Martin was still collecting pay records when he heard the order to prepare to abandon ship. Dragging a bag full of documents, he climbed up to the main deck, hoping to find a boat in which the documents could be safely taken to one of the destroyers. But a quick look around told him that there were few boats left intact. Spotting the wounded being loaded into the number-one motor whaleboat, he dragged the bag across the deck toward the group. After explaining to Doctor Blackwell what the bag contained, he placed the bag in the boat and hurried back to the pay office to rescue several thousand dollars in cash.

As Ensign Martin slipped and stumbled along the foam-slickened main deck, the fourth P-40 crashed into the sea alongside the stricken ship. The word had not reached the flight deck, and the sailors and airmen were still working like demons to push planes over the side. The next candidate was a fighter parked just abaft the number-four 3-inch gun. The landing gear was still intact, but both tires were flat and the right wing hung down so that the tip dragged on the deck. Though it was the best choice, the P-40 obviously was not going to be easy to move, and Divoll told the exhausted men to take a break.

Throughout the ship the men were relaxing their efforts. The list, the fires, and the fact that the *Langley* had been dead in the water for nearly an hour made it evident that the order to abandon ship would soon be given. There were also other signs that the *Langley* was about to be abandoned.

Charles Snay and Ensign J. Thurman, the crypto officer, were preparing code books and other publications for destruction, and Radioman First Class George Copeland had been sent below to get the items that the radio room crew wanted to take with them. Similar preparations were going on all over the ship.

Though their efforts had been relaxed or redirected, there was still plenty of energy being exerted to save the ship. Even after Ensign Emmanuel had released his weary men, about half had remained on the poop deck, continuing to fight the fire. On the flight deck the sailors and pilots were still struggling to push planes off the deck.

In the engine room the effort to save the ship had reached its limit. The fire room decks were awash, water was knee-deep in the engine room, and at the throttle control it had risen to four feet. Lieutenant Frey sent word to the bridge that there was no hope of

Chester (left) and Norman (right) Koepsell were inseparable. The brothers patched leak after leak in a futile effort to stem the flow of water that flooded the engine room. Both survived and were the only *Langley* crewmen to be assigned to the new *Langley* (CVL-27). (Photo courtesy of Chester Koepsell)

righting the ship or restarting the motors—the ship was lost. Acting on his own, Frey started sending the men who were not absolutely needed up to the main deck. The Koepsell brothers were among those who remained with the chief engineer in the rapidly flooding engine room.[26]

The sudden appearance of the engine room personnel on deck provoked more men to go over the side. The large number of people scrambling over the rail and jumping into the water caused the men on the *Whipple* to think that the order to abandon ship had been given aboard the *Langley*. The *Whipple* log records: "1325 *Langley* crew abandon ship; began picking up survivors."

Lieutenant Frey's messenger reached the bridge at 1330. The captain listened to the report, asked one or two questions, and looked aft at the smoking, listing ship. A P-40 slowly upended, somersaulted, and crashed heavily into the sea. It was the fifth and last plane that was pushed over in the futile attempt to correct the list. Some smoke still poured from the stern and from beneath the flight deck. Heavy objects, wreckage, and small loose material were spilling from the port side into the sea. At 1332 Commander McConnell concluded that the ship was lost and ordered her abandoned.[27]

CHAPTER 6

The *Langley* Abandoned

The order to abandon ship spread quickly. It was followed by a landslide rush over the sides and a remarkably efficient rescue operation performed by the *Edsall* and *Whipple*. The entire episode lasted just twenty-six minutes from the time Commander Mc-Connell ordered abandon ship to the time the last man was pulled aboard the *Whipple*.[1] The speed with which the rescue was accomplished resulted from ideal sea conditions and the fully justified fear that more Japanese bombers would soon appear. Another factor that made the rescue a speedy affair was the haste with which the crew left their ship, the result of a widely held belief that the *Langley* would roll over at any minute. This belief, based on the ship's 18-degree list, was supported by rumors of torpedo hits and massive port-side flooding.[2]

In fact, though hard hit, the ship was sinking very slowly. The water that was rising in the engine room and the forward compartments was entering through relatively small, though numerous, opening in the hull. The *Langley* did not have extensive watertight compartmenting, due in part to her interior design and in part to the fact that all the modifications had been done during periods of budget austerity. Therefore, the water flowed fairly easily from one compartment to the other. But the *Langley* was tightly sealed along the main deck. As the water rose inside the hull, the air trapped between the rising water and the main deck compressed, slowing the inflow of water. The ship was, of course, not airtight, but the slow rate at which the air escaped substantially reduced the rate at which the water entered.[3] Unknown to the crewmen who were hurriedly leaving the ship, in her present condition the *Langley* would float for several hours.

Given enough time the *Langley* would certainly sink, but there was now little likelihood that she would burn or that the fires would reach the aviation gasoline stored beneath the bridge structure. Enormous credit must be given to the *Langley* crewmen who had fought the stubborn, dangerous fires under truly adverse conditions. Now, as the crew went over the sides, the fires were either out or under control. In some parts of the ship, the fires that still burned created thick clouds of black smoke, making the situation appear far more serious than it really was. But for the most part, there was little smoke to hamper the men or to suggest that the ship was in immediate danger of being blown out of the water.

As the men jumped or lowered themselves down knotted lines to the water, the *Langley*'s escorts moved in to pick them up. The *Whipple* to starboard and the *Edsall* to port had already made preparations, their hulls rigged with cargo nets, ladders, and knotted lines. Boats had been lowered and booms extended out from the decks with more lines trailing in the water.

On the *Langley* there was some confusion, as is to be expected, but no panic. A few men returned to their quarters to obtain valued possessions, usually watches, wallets, and cameras. Others tried, but were prevented by fire or flooding. Someone, probably a gunner's mate, had deposited two piles of small arms on the main deck from which several men took pistols but ignored the heavier rifles and BARs.

Nearly everyone wore a life jacket, and the few who did not apparently felt that the distance to the destroyers was so short that a life jacket was not really needed. The main deck was crowded—most people going over the starboard rail and lowering themselves down the sloping hull to the water. After the ferocity and terror of the attack and the dramatic scenes played out during the firefighting period, the abandonment was anticlimactic. It was not, however, without its highlights.

Excitement, and near tragedy, occurred only moments after the order to abandon ship had been given. On the starboard side just abaft the bridge structure, the number-one motor whaleboat

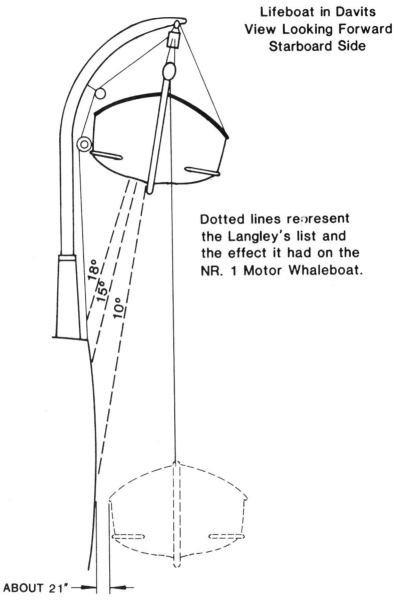

**Lifeboat in Davits
View Looking Forward
Starboard Side**

**Dotted lines represent
the Langley's list and
the effect it had on the
NR. 1 Motor Whaleboat.**

18°
15°
10°

ABOUT 21"

The effect of the *Langley*'s list from 0°–18° to port.

hung in its davits, filled with the most seriously wounded men, including Lieutenant Bailey, and a small crew of attending pharmacists. How the boat was to be lowered with the *Langley* listing 18 degrees is not explained in any report or recalled by the survivors. For even when the ship was on an even keel, the boat only cleared the hull by about twenty-one inches.[4] Even a 10-degree list would have kept the boat from swinging away from the strongback when released, and would have caused the boat to strike the edge of the deck when it was lowered. An 18-degree list would cause the boat to swing slightly inboard and drag heavily against the hull as it dropped. Under those circumstances the boat would have a strong tendency to roll outboard as it slid down the hull, a situation that could easily result in an upset.

All those potential problems were cast aside when without warning the after fall parted. The stern plunged down, the boat striking the *Langley*'s sloping hull and rolling outboard. Pharmacists and wounded were pitched out of the upended boat into the water. Quickly, the men on deck let go the forward fall allowing the heavy boat to bounce and skid down the hull, striking the water.

The unfortunate men had hardly hit the water when dozens of able-bodied men leaped to their rescue. Among the rescuers was Bernard Jasper, who had just emerged from the radio room when the whaleboat fell. Without hesitation, Jasper bounded across the deck and vaulted over the rail to the water twenty feet below. Around him the wounded were calling for help, many unable to comprehend through the haze of shock and morphine what had suddenly gone wrong. There were a few who floated as though lifeless in their kapok life jackets. From the deck above, the men were shouting and pointing in an effort to direct the rescuers to the floundering wounded.

The boat had landed upright in the water, and several sailors slid down the forward fall into the boat. Casting off, they floated the boat among the struggling swimmers and started pulling the sodden wounded aboard. The rescue was completed with surprising speed, and the rescuers hoped they had gotten all the wounded back into the boat. In fact one man had been missed.

The near disaster had been caused by battle damage to the after fall that had either been cut by shrapnel or partially burned through. The list had added to the problem just as it was adding to other problems throughout the ship.

When the *Langley* was on an even keel, her flight deck was fifty-six feet above the water. But the list had raised the deck on the high side to about sixty-four feet, while the low side dropped to about forty-eight feet above the water. Few sailors had had any intention of jumping from either side of the flight deck, and several watched with slack-jawed amazement when one man jumped feet first, ramrod straight, off the high side with his flat "tin-hat" securely strapped on.

The man who jumped was Fireman First Class Brown who had been on the number-one 3-inch gun with Marvin Snyder. Brown went off the high side and fell like a stone into the water sixty-four feet below. Even with his heavy life jacket on, his momentum carried him below the surface so that the flat skirt of his helmet acted as an effective drogue brake. The drag caused by the helmet was enormous and would have broken Brown's neck had the chin strap not parted at the crucial moment. Even so, the fortunate Brown later told his friend Snyder, "It stretched my neck a little."[5]

Ensign Ditto and Howard Whan sat on the flight deck, their legs dangling over the edge. They were watching other men make their decisions on how and where to abandon ship, and discussing what they were going to do. Many swimmers had already reached the *Whipple*, and from their elevated position Ditto and Whan could look down on the destroyer's deck and watch the men climb aboard.

"What are you going to do?" the torpedoman asked the officer.

"I'm going over the side," answered Ditto, looking down at the water, over sixty feet below.

"From up here?"

"Sure. Go feet first and it won't hurt you," the ensign said, and suddenly pushed himself off the edge.[6]

Whan watched the ensign as he shot downward, feet and legs together, elbows pressed tightly against his life jacket, balled fists clenched against his chest. Ditto hit the water with a tremendous splash, popped to the surface and started swimming strongly toward the *Whipple*.

Deciding that if Ditto could do it so could he, Whan pushed himself off the edge. As soon as he left the deck, he knew he was in trouble. Instead of falling feet first, Whan was tilted slightly backwards. When he hit the water it felt like his insides had been torn apart, and there was a searing pain at the base of his spine. Gasping for breath, Whan lay partially stunned in the water, the warm, salty taste of blood in his mouth. Regaining his breath, and suppressing his initial fear, Whan found that he was able to swim and painfully started toward the *Whipple.*

In the nearly deserted engine room, Lieutenant Frey, Machinist Butts, and the Koepsell brothers stood knee-deep in oily sea water, braced against the ship's list. Water still spurted from a dozen leaks, and occasionally a control panel would short out as seawater touched its circuits. From the fire room came the hissing sound of steam rushing from the popped safety valves. Suddenly a messenger clattered down the ladder with the order to abandon ship, and Chester and his brother Norman lost no time leaving the engine room. Entering the mess hall they turned down a corridor that ran along the port side past the brig. As they ran past the darkened cells, they were unaware that a man was locked inside.[7]

The *Langley*'s brig had two cells situated on the port side of the poop deck near the break of the poop. Above the cells and slightly outboard was the stack sponson on which the fourth bomb had exploded. Throughout the attack and during the hour-long fight to save the ship, a sailor had remained confined in one of the cells. His presence there was an oversight that was still uncorrected as the ship was being abandoned.

When the ship had started to list and the cell filled with acrid smoke, the frightened sailor beat on the door and shouted to attract attention. No one came. At 1315 the ship's power had been momentarily disrupted, plunging the cell into blackness.[8] Fifteen minutes later, the now-terrified man heard shouts to abandon ship. He could hear men running and shouting, some very close. Panic seized him when he realized that he was being left behind, and he doubled his efforts to attract attention. Still no one came.

There was a faint similarity between the man trapped in the brig and Earl Snyder who was still trapped in his cast. Both men needed help to get out. In Snyder's case there was plenty of help around him since the main deck was crowded with sailors. But his thought processes were only working part time, and he stumbled on ignoring the obvious and seeking the indefinite. What he sought was something with which to break off the plaster, and he finally found it in the mess hall.

Sitting on the deck, Snyder shoved a broken chair leg under the edge of his cast and tried to pry it off. His efforts were largely ineffectual because he was too weak and uncoordinated to break the thick plaster.

"Hey! What are you doing?" asked a sailor who had apparently come into the mess hall to find something to eat.

"I'm trying to get this goddamn cast off," slurred Snyder. "Give me a hand."

"You'll kill yourself doin' that," argued the sailor.

"I'll sure as hell kill myself if I try swimmin' with this goddamn sinker on," Snyder answered, while continuing to twist the chair leg under the cast.

"Ok, buddy, it's your life. Gimme that thing," the sailor said as he took the chair leg from Snyder.

Because the plaster had not fully set up the cast came apart fairly easily, and with surprisingly little pain to Snyder. But without the cast he was virtually helpless and could not move without assistance. The sailor found a life jacket, and helped by a second man they carried Snyder to the starboard side and eased him down to the water. A motor whaleboat from the *Whipple*, attracted by the shouts of the swimmers supporting Snyder, hurried in their direction.

Inasmuch as Snyder had to be lowered to the water, it would seem that the task could have been more easily accomplished from the lower, port side. That is probably true, but wreckage was sliding off the decks making the water along the port side hazardous. The danger of being hit by stuff falling off the ship kept many men from going off that side, while others were afraid that the ship might roll over on them before they could swim clear. Those concerns explain why the majority of the crew made their escape over the high side despite the longer drop to the water. There were, however, men who dragged their heels about going over either side, and the reason for this had nothing to do with falling objects or long drops. Their reluctance was the normal reaction of men who cannot swim.

George Vano stood at the starboard rail with the bakers Wetherbee, Riley, and McLean who were urging him to go down one of the knotted lines. They assured him that his life jacket would keep him afloat and that they would be there to help him all the way across to the *Whipple*, now just fifty yards away.[10]

Finally Vano resigned himself to his fate and agreed to go over the side, preceded by Wetherbee who lowered himself down a knotted line, dropping the final distance to the water. Looking up, Wetherbee saw Vano clutching the end of the line about fifteen feet above the water, refusing to let go. The chief had apparently made a last-minute decision to back out of the deal, and the men coming down the line above Vano were shouting at him to let go.

"I can't swim," shouted the unhappy chief.

"You better learn," yelled the man above him, "cause I'm coming down!"

The sailor dropped onto Vano knocking the chief off the line and into the water. Terrified, Vano thrashed about until he realized that his life jacket really worked, though as later events would show, he did not remain convinced.

Chief Vano's experience provided a touch of comic relief to what was really a very depressing scene. But among those who missed the chief's departure, there were also a few who got at least a smile from some of the things they saw. David Jones was amused when he spotted the horseshoe-shaped taffrail from Mealley's motor launch draped around the formast. Jones, however, missed one of the most memorable events that attended the *Langley*'s sinking.

In the pay office a series of events was starting to unfold that has developed into one of the legends nearly every *Langley* survivor relates. Even those who were unaware of the occurrence at the time have some version of what happened. The details vary, usually slightly and occasionally wildly, but all describe "thousands of dollars" that floated on the water along the *Langley*'s starboard side.[11]

Immediately after placing the rough rolls and cash books in the number-one whaleboat, Ensign Martin went to the pay office where several thousand dollars in Phillippine, Dutch, and Australian money were locked in two safes. The money was essentially the ship's payroll, and Ensign Martin was one of those responsible for it.

Assisted by Seaman Second Class Dorsey Elkins, Martin opened both safes and removed approximately sixty thousand dollars, placing the money in a leather postman-type bag. At the same time, he removed the pay records and put them in the leather pouches with the money. He and Elkins went to the starboard side of the main deck where Martin left the seaman with the money-filled bag. The ensign returned to the pay office and found Pay Clerk A. J. Randall also stuffing money into leather pouches. Ensign Martin left the pay office and went to his quarters on the boat deck where he opened a small safe and removed two thousand dollars that he stuffed into a pillow case.

In the meantime, Randall had come onto the main deck from the pay office with nearly one hundred thousand dollars in two bags. He saw John Kennedy standing at the port rail talking to another yeoman, Richard Ratajik. Kennedy and Ratajik, who were both crap players, were trying to convince one another to go below and retrieve their own money from their lockers.

"I'll give you two hundred dollars if you'll go down to my locker and get my money," said Kennedy.

"How much money you got down there?" asked Ratajik.

"Eight hundred," answered Kennedy. Ratajik laughed, and said "I got twelve hundred and I'll give you three hundred to get mine."

Before they could finish their haggling, clerk Randall dragged his bags to where they were standing and said, "Here, one of you take one of these, the other take the other."

The bags were open at the top and the two yeoman were flabbergasted at the amount of money they saw inside. Neither knew the exact amount but it was obviously a lot. Ordering both men to jump into the water, Randall dropped the bags to them. Looking quickly around, Kennedy spotted a chair floating near by and grabbed it. Wedging the bag between the four legs he started swimming toward the *Edsall*, pushing the treasure-laden chair ahead of him.

Having disposed of that money, the pay clerk returned to the pay office and filled a third bag with money. Going to the starboard rail, he apparently threw it to someone who was already in the water. The bag must not have been securely closed, because as it arced out from the ship and started down, it broke open raining Australian currency on the swimmers below.

John Kennedy (third from left) saved over $50,000 from the sinking *Langley*. Kennedy was cited for bravery and later commissioned under the V-7 program. He is shown here in New Guinea. (Photo courtesy of John Kennedy)

Thomas Spence had been picked up by a motor whaleboat from the *Whipple* and was propped up in the bow facing aft toward the *Langley* when he saw Randall appear at the rail and throw the bag overboard. As the money, bundled in small packets, hit the water many of the swimmers grabbed it.

Earl Snyder was painfully struggling in the water waiting for the *Whipple*'s boat when bundles of money and loose bills rained down on him. One of the men near him grabbed a bundle and shoved it under his life jacket, but Snyder ignored the windfall, saying later, "I was worrying about Snyder, not money."

Walter Sinner was swimming on his back toward the destroyer, facing the *Langley*, when he saw Randall hurl the money bag away from the ship. The cash fell into the water behind him, but Sinner gave no thought to going back for it. As he swam slowly away from the soggy treasure, he saw many of those on whom the money had fallen scooping bills out of the water.

Reginald Mills, who had manned a machine gun on the bridge, also saw Randall throw the bag and was in a perfect position to gather the money as it floated on the surface. Like Snyder, he was more interest in survival than in cash and later said, "I didn't think I'd ever have a chance to spend it anyway." Little did he know that his grim assessment of the situation would soon be even closer to the truth.

Carl Onberg was another swimmer who saw the action as it happened, but ignored the money as did many others. In fact, those who were not interested in the floating cash greatly outnumbered those who literally grabbed at the opportunity. Many more were totally unaware that the episode had happened until they heard the story later aboard the *Whipple*.

Lester Bates was one of those who took advantage of the unexpected dividend. Stuffing the bundled cash under his life jacket and inside his dungaree shirt, he collected about five hundred pounds in Australian notes before resuming his swim toward the *Whipple*. After he had been pulled aboard the destroyer and had gone below, he ran into an old friend who was a fireman aboard the *Whipple*. Bates told him about the money incident and showed him the cash he had grabbed. Then out of friendship, Bates gave half of the money to his friend, an act of generosity that would benefit Bates and his shipmates several days later—those that survived.

While Pay Clerk Randall was trying to send thousands of dollars across to the destroyer and scattering a small part of it on the water, Ensign Martin was completing his own efforts to save the ship's money and pay records. He returned to the main deck and found Elkins waiting patiently with the bag containing sixty thousand dollars and many of the pay records. By the time Martin and Elkins went over the starboard rail the ship was nearly deserted. The money that had caused so much excitement had disappeared, mostly floating away or sinking. Both Martin and Elkins swam to the *Whipple*, safely delivering sixty-two thousand dollars in cash.

More important things than money were being thrown over the side, but there was no intention that they be caught and taken to the destroyer. They were placed in weighted bags, securely fastened so as not to come open and leave their contents floating on the surface. At various levels in the bridge structure officers were destroying or disposing of the ship's sensitive documents. Code books, publications, charts and log books splashed into the water and sank quickly out of sight. In the crypto room all the code machines were smashed with a fire axe. Of all the acts performed on any warship, none symbolizes her defeat with greater finality than does the destruction of the ship's documents.

There is a series of events that attends the sinking of most ships that is poetically similar to the dying of a living creature. A ship dies slowly—life flowing out of her in progressive stages. As she settles, machinery, blowers, and generators progressively cease to function and the crew abandons her. When the last man leaves, the ship dies. The *Langley* was very nearly dead.

Most of the crew was gone. A few were delaying their departure for a variety of personal reasons, others were still at their posts performing their duty to the last. Commander McConnell was on the signal bridge, while below decks, officers and chiefs were making sure that the men had all gotten out. In the generator room, Jim Harvey and Fireman Second Class William Bowers were told to shut down and abandon ship. Calmly the men shut down the generators according to routine and left the compartment. As the generators whirred to a stop, the lights dimmed and went out. The *Langley* became a darkened, inert hulk.[12]

In the darkness the two men felt their way forward along the narrow passageway. Emerging onto the well deck they found the ship nearly deserted save for a few men, mostly officers and petty officers. Two decks above and behind them Ensign Emmanuel was completing a tour of the area to be sure that all his people had gotten away. As he descended to the poop deck, the ensign ran into a master-at-arms.

"Have you checked the brig?" asked Emmanuel. There was a moment of stunned silence before the man answered. "Oh my God!" he exclaimed and ran forward.[13]

Shortly the master-at-arms returned to tell Emmanuel that the prisoner had been released and appeared to be unhurt, though "damned scared." Satisfied that his area was clear, the wounded ensign abandoned ship.

The water between the *Langley* and the two destroyers was still filled with splashing swimmers, though the greater concentrations were nearer the destroyers than the tender. Boats from the destroyers were picking up the weaker swimmers, and a motor whaleboat that had come from the *Langley* was stopped in the water about one-third of the way between the tender and the *Edsall*. The *Langley*'s boat was the number-two motor whaleboat that had hung in davits on the tender's port side just forward of the flight deck. How the boat had survived the explosion and fire from the second and third bomb hits is beyond explanation. Also beyond explanation is the discovery that caused the boat to be stopped where it was.

Army Lieutenants Akerman and Dix had for some reason decided not to get into the number-one motor whaleboat with the other wounded. But they had watched the loading and launching operations, and the unexpected upset. As the occupants were spilled out, Dix clearly saw the badly wounded gunnery officer, Lieutenant Bailey, pitch out of the boat and tumble into the sea. While the wounded were being rescued, the two pilots, with no clearly defined plan for leaving the ship, started walking aft.

What they did during the next several minutes is not known. Dix, partially numbed by morphine, recalls only a few highlights, and Akerman is dead. The next thing that Dix clearly recalls is finding a group of sailors trying to launch the undamaged number-two motor whaleboat on the port side. The airmen climbed into the boat with several sailors and were lowered to the water. As the boat touched the water Fireman First Class Raymond Shepston slid down the forward fall into the boat, the last man to board before the whaleboat shoved off.[14]

As the whaleboat chugged slowly toward the *Edsall*, the sailors pulled aboard anyone that was near enough to be grabbed. Seeing the boat, many swimmers hailed it, and in every case the helm was put over and the boat went to the swimmer. As a result, the trip from the *Langley* to the *Edsall* was slow, and the boat was filling to capacity.

During one of the many course changes, a man was seen floating motionless on the water, supported by his kapok life jacket, head back. The man's inactivity was enough to make him stand out among the thrashing swimmers and cause alarm. Turning away from a swimmer, the boat headed toward the motionless man while two sailors prepared to drag him aboard. As the boat slid alongside the limp figure, one of the men exclaimed, "Jesus! It's Lieutenant Bailey!"

Unconscious, badly wounded, and dying, the gunnery officer was pulled into the crowded whaleboat and laid out on the floor. Finding the lieutenant in the water on the port side after he had been dumped in the water on the starboard side baffled those who had seen the earlier accident. He certainly did not swim there. Equally baffling was how he had been overlooked when the wounded were being rescued and put back into the number-one motor whaleboat. The answer would never be learned. Lieutenant Bailey remained unconscious and died the following day.[15]

While the number-two motor whaleboat hurried to the *Edsall* with its grisly find, the last men were leaving the *Langley*. Snay was making his way along the lower decks looking for stragglers, surprised at how quiet the ship was. He had expected the old tender at least to creak and groan as she settled. Instead, there was nearly total silence, broken only by his footfalls and an occasional shout from someone who was also looking for stragglers.

On the main deck Harvey and Bowers had joined a handful of sailors at the starboard rail amidships. Commander McConnell came toward them, and seeing that they were making no move to leave the ship ordered them over the rail. He stood by while they carried out the order.

Harvey swung himself over the rail, hung by his hands and then let go. He slid quickly down the sloping hull and splashed into the water with comparative ease. It was only a short distance to the *Whipple*, and there were few men still in the water. While he swam, encumbered by the bulky kapok life jacket, Harvey saw several thick bundles of Australian five-pound notes floating on the surface. At another time the money might have interested him, but now he felt much like a man who was about to miss the bus. He swam through the money and was soon aboard the destroyer.

Behind Harvey a boat from the *Whipple* bumped against the

"1358 completed rescue work . . ." In the background is the destroyer USS *Edsall* (DD-217), which has also completed the rescue operation. This is probably the last picture ever taken of her. Two days later she was lost with all hands. (U.S. Navy)

Langley's hull. On the main deck Commander McConnell was joined by the few officers and petty officers who had remained to be sure that everyone was off. Satisfied that those who could had escaped, McConnell ordered the men into the waiting boat. When the last man was gone, the captain followed.[16]

At 1358, just thirty-three minutes after the first man had abandoned the *Langley* during the premature rush, the *Whipple* fished the last man out of the water. There were now 308 officers and men from the tender jammed into the narrow confines of the old four-piper. Most had been sent below to reduce top weight but several remained on the destroyer's deck. On the *Langley*'s far side the *Edsall* had already taken aboard the last survivor that had gone over the *Langley*'s port rail.

There now developed a rather awkward situation—the *Langley* did not seem to be sinking. At 1428 the *Whipple* pumped nine 4-inch rounds into the hull without any noticeable effect. Four minutes later she launched a torpedo that hit just abaft the starboard jib crane. Instead of sinking, the *Langley* slowly righted until she was almost back on an even keel. The *Whipple* moved around to the port side and fired another torpedo that hit her below the stack sponson. The second torpedo hit had a more apparent effect. A tremendous explosion was quickly followed by a fierce fire that erupted at the break of the poop deck and spread aft, engulfing

"At 1428 fired 9 rounds 4″/50 cal. common ammunition into hulk, followed by 1 torpedo at 1432 . . ." (This photo taken from the *Whipple* is courtesy of Lawrence Divoll.)

"... and another at 1445." (Photo courtesy of Lawrence Divoll)

the entire after part of the ship. Burning hotly, the *Langley* settled and was soon very low in the water.[17]

By now there was a real concern that the Japanese would return any minute. The destroyer skippers, Lieutenant Commander Eugene S. Karpe on the *Whipple* and Lieutenant J. J. Nix on the *Edsall*, were reluctant to hang around any longer, and for very good reasons. Both ships were inadequately equipped with antiaircraft defense, both suffered from prior battle damage, and both were filled to over capacity with the *Langley* survivors. Their anxiety was shared by Commander E. M. Crouch, commanding officer of Destroyer Division 57, who was on board the *Whipple*. At 1446 both destroyers cleared the area.[18]

As the destroyers disappeared over the horizon, the *Langley* was still afloat and burning. No one saw the old "Covered Wagon" go down, a fact that caused a short-lived controversy. But despite the small controversy surrounding her unobserved sinking, her end was in a way fitting. The *Langley* had been a pioneer, and like so many pioneers she died alone.

CHAPTER 7

Out of the Frying Pan into the Fire

Bumper to bumper trucks and long columns of shouting, cursing soldiers choked the streets leading to Tjilatjap's harbor. The docks were jammed with men—some streaming aboard ships, some waiting, and some pleading for space. Unable to reach the docks because of the unbelievable traffic jam, many units had turned back and collided with others that were pushing into the city. The result was chaos, as NCOs and officers became separated from their men and soldiers of four nations were mixed into a leaderless mob.[1]

For several days soldiers had been swarming into Java's only remaining port in a desperate bid to get out of Java before the Japanese landed. By 27 February it was clear to everyone but the Dutch that Java could not be successfully defended, and the Allied withdrawal was in full swing. But for the captains of the few ships remaining in the harbor, there was a more immediate reason for wanting to leave.

Despite frequent air-raid warnings, Tjilatjap had not yet been bombed. But the captains were fully aware that the Japanese had already neutralized the huge navy base at Surabaja and had pounded Darwin into a smoking ruin. It was frighteningly evident to the ships' captains that the Japanese would not leave Tjilatjap unmolested much longer.

Commander E. Paul Abernethy, captain of the fleet oiler USS *Pecos* (AO-6), had especially good reason for wanting to get his ship out to sea. He knew that when the air raids came, the *Pecos*, the only fleet oiler in the Netherlands East Indies, would receive special attention.[2] Even if the Japanese missed the oiler, there was a near certainty that a fleeing ship would be sunk in Tjilatjap's narrow, twisting channel, blocking the channel and trapping the *Pecos* inside.

Since 6 February the *Pecos* had been in Tjilatjap receiving fuel oil from bulk tankers and pumping it into Dutch, British, and American warships. As the Japanese juggernaut rolled down toward Java, Commander Abernethy had gone daily to ABDA-FLOAT headquarters and pleaded to be allowed to leave. The commander wanted to continue his duties as a fleet tanker at sea, and not remain bottled up in the doomed harbor.

Commander Abernethy's idea was endorsed by Admiral Glassford, who wanted to lift bunker oil from the stock ashore into the *Pecos* and send her to sea. That procedure appeared to the admiral to be "more desirable than to require our ships to fuel at Tjilatjap under constant threat of air attack while immobilized."[3] Abernethy

Commander E. Paul Abernethy, shown here as a rear admiral, was the captain of the *Pecos*. He was awarded the Navy Cross for his actions on 1 March 1942. (Photo courtesy of E. Paul Abernethy)

and Glassford were, of course, correct in their belief that the *Pecos* would be more effective at sea, but the Dutch refused to agree to the plan.

Dutch intransigence on the issue of oil had become a daily problem to Admiral Glassford. He later wrote:

> The whole situation with regard to fuel oil was in truth becoming exceedingly critical. Especially did we view as unfortunate that no effort had been made to lift some 50,000 tons of oil out of Surabaja, in spite of repeated recommendations that this be done. The Dutch really never gave up hope that Java could be defended successfully until it fell at their feet like a house of cards. It was impossible to persuade them that the oil should be removed to a place of safety from Java.

On 20 February Admiral Glassford made arrangements to send a tanker to Surabaja in an attempt to lift "at least some oil from there." He had a choice of sending the *Pecos* or a civilian tanker, the *British Judge*, and chose the latter because she was larger and more expendable than the *Pecos*, "a regular naval tanker equipped to fuel vessels at sea."

The *British Judge* returned to Tjilatjap fully loaded with oil on the 24th, and was ordered to pump her cargo into the *Pecos*. After the transfer had been completed, the *Pecos* was to clear the port and proceed to a prescribed rendezvous at sea. But for a reason that was never explained to Admiral Glassford, the Dutch in Tjilatjap ignored the order, and the oil from the *British Judge* was discharged into shore tanks. Thus, during the days when Commander Abernethy was desperate to get his ship to sea, valuable time was lost through Dutch shortsightedness. The delay proved to be fatal for most of the oiler's crew.

The *Pecos*'s chance to escape came with the word of the *Langley*'s expected arrival. The dock to which the tanker was tied was needed to offload the *Langley*'s thirty-two P-40s, and Commander Abernethy was ordered to make room. On the morning of 27 February the *Pecos* got under way, and after a brief delay caused by an air-raid alarm, proceeded out Tjilatjap's narrow, twisting channel to the open sea.

Commander Abernethy was not kidding himself or anybody else about the *Pecos*'s chance of escaping, since he knew that a

Japanese carrier force was already operating in the Indian Ocean. Two days earlier he had refused to accept any wounded passengers who were not ambulatory and could not take care of themselves. His decision saved the lives of the men he had refused to take. Another example of how dimly he viewed the chance for escape had occurred that same day when he had ordered a large number of bamboo poles brought aboard and lashed to the upper decks. The poles, a grim reminder of the danger that lay ahead, were intended to provide flotation for swimmers if the ship were sunk. In order to improve whatever small chance he did have to escape, Abernethy had refused to join a 10-knot convoy on departure day. Doing so, he believed, would lengthen the time his ship would be subject to Japanese air attack. Events canceled that decision.[4]

As soon as his ship was out of the channel, Commander Abernethy set her course for Ceylon, and doubled the lookouts. He then ordered all hatches closed, the dogs set wrench-tight, and had a steam blanket laid across all the oil tanks. The last measure was a precaution against fire and explosion if the ship were attacked—a very large possibility.

The concern for his ship, the decision to take bamboo poles aboard, and the refusal to accept any nonambulatory wounded reflect the qualities that made Captain Abernethy an exceptional officer. An Annapolis graduate, Abernethy was described by fellow officers as a fine seaman who exhibited level-headed practicality and rock-like stability under pressure. The enlisted men knew him less well, but he was respected for his obvious competence and the fact that he was not an over-zealous disciplinarian. One crewman remarked, "He was a true gentleman."[5]

Three hours out of Tjilatjap the *Pecos* copied some of the *Langley*'s last radio transmissions giving the tender's position and condition, and within half an hour word was received that the *Langley* survivors were being picked up by the *Edsall* and the *Whipple*. At that time the *Pecos* was barely thirty miles from the scene of the bombing, much too close, and Commander Abernethy "proceeded west at maximum speed."[6]

One hour later the *Pecos*'s dash for safety was blocked by an order from COMSOWESPAC directing her to proceed to Christmas Island, about 260 nautical miles south-east of Tjilatjap. There she was to meet the *Edsall* and *Whipple*, take aboard survivors, and then proceed to Exmouth Gulf on Australia's west coast. The surviving Army personnel, who had been aboard the *Langley*, however, were still committed to their mission despite the fact that they had no planes to fly.

In what must rank as one of the monumentally stupid decisions of World War II, the airmen were to be put aboard the *Edsall* and taken to Java, where they would fight as infantry.[7] This was to be done at a time when American, British, and Australian personnel were already leaving Java by whatever means was available, and it was obvious that the Japanese could not be prevented from taking the island.

While the *Pecos* was steaming toward Christmas Island, the last act in the failing attempt to bolster Java's fighter strength was being played out in Tjilatjap. Second Lieutenant Jim Moorehead, one of the few remaining pilots of the 17th Pursuit Squadron, had been

First Lieutenant James Moorehead was a fighter pilot with the 17th Pursuit Squadron in Java. He had been sent to Tjilatjap to lead Lieutenant Keenan's green replacements to Blimbing. He returned to Blimbing empty-handed in time to burn his own P-40 and catch the last B-17 out of Java. (Photo courtesy of James Moorehead)

sent to Tjilatjap to lead the replacements back to the squadron's base at Blimbing. Getting off an ancient narrow-gauge train, Moorehead pushed his way through milling soldiers and snarled military traffic until he reached the long pier that the *Pecos* had vacated just a few hours earlier.

There were dozens of people standing around on the dock, but none of them could tell Moorehead anything about the *Langley*. Unable to locate any officials or anyone who knew when the tender was scheduled to arrive, he turned his attention to a nearby warehouse office. The office was jammed with men, and more were crowded around the door, all trying to find transportation for their units out of Java. While standing at the back of the tightly packed group, Moorehead was approached by an American reporter for the Chicago *Sun Times*.

"You're Army Air Force, aren't you?" The reporter asked.[8]

"That's right."

"You down here to meet the *Langley*?"

"Yea, but nobody can tell me when she's getting in," complained Moorehead.

"Well I got some bad news for you. There'll be no *Langley*. The Japs got her." The reporter lowered his voice indicating the finality of the statement.

The news was no surprise to Moorehead, who had started having doubts when he saw the empty dock. There was no official confirmation of the reporter's story, but as Moorehead pushed his way back toward the train station he heard a lot of talk about the sinking. An hour later he was on his way back to Blimbing.

The hopelessness of the *Langley*'s mission, even had she delivered her deck load of fighters, was dramatically demonstrated thirty-six hours later when the 17th Pursuit Squadron burned their last six planes and caught the last B-17 out of Java.[9]

While Moorehead was learning that he had made his trip to Tjilatjap for nothing, the *Pecos* was steaming toward Christmas Island. The trip took about seventeen uneventful hours, during which Commander Abernethy made ready to receive the survivors. His crew, normally 125, was already swollen to more than twice that number by survivors from the *Houston*, *Marblehead*, and *Stewart* who had been taken aboard in Tjilatjap.[10] The skipper recalled

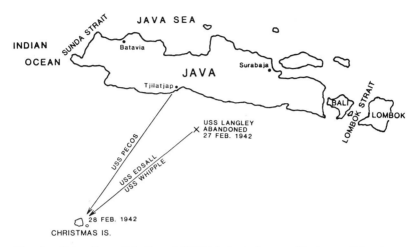

Tracks of the *Pecos*, *Edsall*, and *Whipple* from Java to Christmas Island.

that the *Langley* had a crew of about 500 men, which meant that the *Pecos* was going to be a very crowded ship. But the crowding was less a concern to the captain than was the increasing threat of air attack. If the Japanese jumped them after the transfer was made, the loss of life would be enormous.

The place chosen for the rendezvous was Flying Fish Cove on the island's north side. There a British mining firm, the Christmas Island Phosphate Company, had built a small harbor facility that included a dock, administrative buildings, and a radio station. It appears, however, that the presence of those limited facilities was not the reason that the site was selected. It seems, instead, that the island was picked because it was reasonably close, and provided a small lee against the wind that blew across thousands of miles of open sea.

By 0820 on 28 February, the destroyers were steaming slowly back and forth near the harbor entrance waiting for the *Pecos*. Shortly after their arrival, a company employee, Mister E. Craig, had gone out to the *Whipple* in the company's small motor launch to offer his services as a pilot to the warships. Instead, his launch was pressed into service to ferry thirty-two airmen from the *Whipple* to the *Edsall*. He was just completing this task when the tanker arrived.[11]

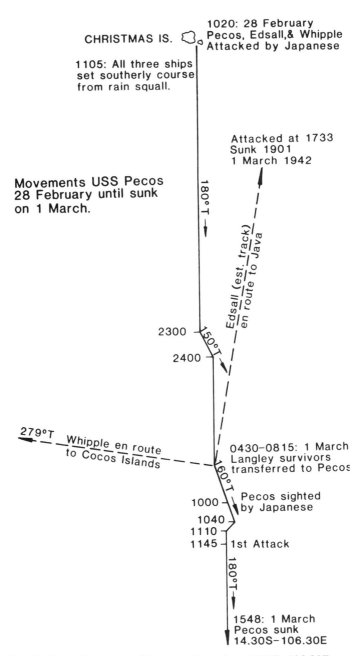

Track of the *Pecos* from Christmas Island to 14.30S–106.30E.

After discharging his last passenger, Craig was asked to take the *Langley*'s first lieutenant, Tom Donovan, from the *Edsall* over to the *Pecos*. Donovan was to go aboard the tanker and work out the details of the transfer with Commander Abernethy. The run from the destroyer to the tanker should have taken ten minutes— Donovan never made it.

Commander Abernethy stood on the port bridge wing watching the small boat as it approached the *Pecos*'s sea ladder. The civilian was standing in the bow and Lieutenant Commander Donovan was seated amidships. There were two native crewmen, one squatting behind Craig and one at the helm. As the boat bumped against the tanker's hull near the sea ladder, an unattended line trailing over the side fouled the propeller.[12]

As the powerless boat drifted away from the *Pecos*, there was a frantic scramble to restart the engine. The boat was still fairly close to the *Pecos* when Craig suddenly jumped from the boat to the tanker's sea ladder. The impetus imparted by his lunge accelerated the boat's drift away from the *Pecos*, the gap widened, and Donovan found himself adrift.

The situation abruptly went from vexing to serious when the clear tropical air suddenly filled with the sounds of roaring airplane engines and exploding bombs. The three American ships were taken completely by surprise. Fortunately for the Americans, the equally surprised Japanese pilots stuck to their planned mission and pasted the phosphate company's dock and radio station instead of going after the three targets of opportunity.

There was consternation on the three ships. Battle alarms sounded, hulls shuddered under the strain of going to full speed, and startled gunners opened up with everyting they had. Like hares bounding for a thicket, the ships sped for cover in a rain squall.

Adrift in the powerless, open boat, Donovan was a stunned spectator to the personal disaster descending on him. Behind him the beach exploded in fountains of sand and flame, and the water was sprinkled with shrapnel from overhead flak bursts and falling debris. In one moment the air around him was filled with violent sounds and frantic movement, and in the next moment the attack was over. The receding ships, the distant gunfire, and the fading sound of engines drove home the awful realization that he had been left behind.

After unloading on the defenseless civilian plant and radio station, two of the planes climbed to 18,000 feet and flew almost directly over the three ships. But having no bombs left to drop, they banked, made a run down the *Pecos*'s starboard side and flew off as the ships entered the safety of the rain squall.[13]

A few miles behind the ships, black smoke rolled skyward from the smashed buildings. At the mouth of the small harbor the launch was again under way, the two native crewmen having finally cleared the fouled line from the propeller. As the boat chugged toward the beach, Donovan scanned the horizon for some sign that the ships were coming back for him. He looked in vain. The next ship he would see would be Japanese, and would mark the beginning of a long, brutal imprisonment.

Thirty minutes after ducking into the rain squall the ships emerged to find the skies empty of all aircraft, and lookouts scanning the horizon for 360 degrees saw nothing. At 1106 the crews secured from air defense quarters.

Commander Edwin M. Crouch, commander of Destroyer Division 57, was the senior officer and the man who would decide the next move. Apparently there was nothing among the factors he considered that suggested any thought of returning to Christmas Island for the unfortunate Donovan. Commander Crouch correctly assumed that the planes had come from the southern tip of Sumatra or from Bali. Because it was still early in the day, and the Japanese pilots had undoubtedly alerted their base about the presence of three United States ships, staying in the area any longer than necessary would have been foolish. Weighing the facts, Commander Crouch felt the best course was to run southward, out of the range of the Japanese land-based bombers, and then transfer the *Langley* survivors at sea.[14] Though undoubtedly correct, the decision angered many of the *Langley* crewmen, who felt that an effort to rescue the very popular first lieutenant of the ship should have been made.

As the ships hurried south the wind increased and the seas became rougher. By evening the sea conditions had not improved and darkness prevented any hope of transfer on 28 February.

Jammed into the destroyer's over-crowded spaces, the *Langley* crewmen prepared to spend another uncomfortable night. The loss of their ship, the crowded conditions, and the abandonment of Lieutenant Commander Donovan were having a serious effect on their morale.

In the *Edsall's* wardroom Army Lieutenants Dix and Akerman found some joy in being reunited with many of their friends from the *Whipple*. Until the other airmen had been transferred from the *Whipple* to the *Edsall* at Christmas Island, Dix and Akerman had been the only airmen aboard the *Edsall*. The reunion brought its disappointments too—eleven airmen were missing.[15] But the biggest disappointment had been the announcement that their fellow pilots and mechanics were being thrown into the lost cause of Java's defense as footsoldiers. Dix and Akerman were lucky in that respect. Because they were wounded, they were to be sent to Australia aboard the *Pecos*.

The wind blew steadily at 26 knots throughout the night, but early in the morning it started to moderate and by 0425 the ships slowed to steerageway and the *Pecos* lowered a forty-foot launch. Boatswain Robert J. Baumker maneuvered the launch through heavy seas and in poor light with such skill that Commander Abernethy later recorded that Baumker "did as fine a job of seamanship in handling the motor launch as I've seen in many a day." But the highest praise for the boatswain's ability came from his peers and is summed up in a statement made by Carl Onberg, "The transfer was made without any sort of difficulty."[16]

Baumker made five trips to the *Whipple* during the next hour and thirty-nine minutes, bringing 276 survivors to the *Pecos*. The wind that had moderated started to pick up again and the seas rose with it, making Baumker's job more difficult and dangerous. The three trips to the *Edsall*, in which 177 men were transferred, required an hour and fifty-one minutes.[17] At 0825 a wet and weary Baumker was back aboard the *Pecos*. During the next twelve hours, the resourceful boatswain would be commended three more times. The last act for which he would be commended would cost him his life.

Having completed the transfer, the three ships parted company. The *Edsall* put about and headed toward Tjilatjap and oblivion. The *Whipple* steadied on course 279 degrees true, upped her speed to 17 knots, and headed for the Cocos Islands where she would refuel from a waiting tanker.[18] The *Pecos* continued south on course 160 degrees true.[19] Ninety minutes later she was slowly drawing out of the range of the Eleventh Air Fleet's bombers, a fact that might have given her captain cause for optimism. In fact, the *Pecos* and her cargo of refugees were about to go from the frying pan into the fire.

Few of the *Langley* survivors were giving much thought to the impending danger. Their relief at having gotten off the crowded destroyers was visible on every face. The tanker afforded them more room, a chance to clean up, and a meal. The men spread themselves out all over the ship, but most of them were grouped on the poop deck, with two other large groups at the base of the bridge structure and under the forecastle. The *Langley* officers were crowded into the tanker's wardroom, and the corridors beneath the poop deck were packed with enlisted "passengers."

Not all the *Langley* survivors were mere passengers. Those with specialties that were in immediate demand were pressed into service to give the *Pecos* crewmen a hand. Bakers, cooks, and mess stewards had hardly set foot on deck before they found themselves at work preparing a quick snack for several hundred exhausted men. At the same time the enormous task of feeding over 700 men a noon meal was started, but few would have a chance to eat it.

Equally busy and hard pressed was the *Langley*'s medical staff of doctors and pharmacist's mates who pitched in to help the *Pecos* medics work on the dozens of wounded men that had come aboard. There were too many wounded to be cared for at once, and they were grouped according to the severity of their injuries. Seaman Second Class Delbert R. Welch had to be operated on at once. While Doctor Blackwell and Lieutenant J. L. Yon, the *Pecos*'s doctor, worked on him, Doctors Handley and Holly, assisted by several pharmacist's mates, tended the men whose problems were serious but less urgent.[20] Among those treated in the second group was Earl Snyder.

Snyder had been cleaned up in the *Whipple*'s sick bay, his broken arm was splinted and his chest wound wrapped. Since that time he had drifted in and out of a morphine haze. Now he found himself lying on a mattress in a passageway, his arm and upper body encased in a fresh cast. Around him lay other men. The blood-encrusted bandages on those who were still waiting their turn contrasted vividly with the neat, white plaster and gauze on those who had already been treated.

As Snyder lay there trying to account for the strange surroundings, he heard a faint, steady sound. The new noise had no direction. It seemed to come through the bulkheads and filled the passageway with a buzzing that slowly grew louder. The sound did not fit the ship, and Snyder strained to hear it. As the sound grew louder Snyder recognized it and felt a surge of adrenalin. He heard an airplane.

The distant drone of the radial engine crept slowly into the consciousness of each *Langley* survivor. Indistinct at first, the volume rose steadily until every man was on his feet, anxiously searching the sky for the sound's source. On the bridge, a lookout spotted a small silver dot far out to port. His shout was quickly followed by the blaring alarm horn that sent the *Pecos* crewmen running to their battle stations, jumping over or crashing through knots of *Langley* men to get there.

In the engine room the general quarters alarm was accompanied by the jangling engine telegraph as the bridge rang down for full speed. Anxious engine-room men opened valves, working the *Pecos*'s twin shafts up to 102 revolutions per minute, until she was straining at 14.6 knots. At that speed her old machinery was not expected to hang together very long.[21]

Every eye on deck strained to identify the strange silver plane from which a series of bright signals flashed. Some men identified the plane as Australian because of the flashed signals. On the bridge every pair of binoculars was trained on the plane and its flashing light while Quartermaster First Class Berry flashed a return challenge.[22]

"I can't read him, captain," said a signalman.

It's a Jap!" Shouted Quartermaster First Class J. Grace. "There are meatballs on his wings."

"Commence firing." Commander Abernethy's order was echoed by his talker Chief Storekeeper L. Saxton. Both 3-inch guns opened up, accompanied by the tanker's ten water-cooled machine guns.

The bark of the 3-inch guns and the clatter of the machine guns sent many *Langley* men diving for cover.

Shepston hit the deck and was almost immediately landed on by someone else. Another man fell across his legs, and a voice near his ear said, "Sorry about that, buddy. Didn't mean to jump on top of ya."[23]

"It's ok. The more cover I get, the better."

For many of the *Langley* men events were starting to unfold like the replay of a bad dream—a single reconnaissance plane at mid-morning with flack bursting far short of the target. The feeling was shared by Commander McConnell and Commander Divoll. Standing with Commander Abernethy on the port bridge wing, they watched the Japanese plane circle twice and fly off.

"We're in for it now," observed Commander McConnell.[24]

Commander Abernethy, having recognized the plane as a carrier-based type, recalled the earlier warning about a Japanese carrier group operating in the Indian Ocean. He later told the press, "I felt we were in for serious trouble."[25] Both officers were, of course, right.

The officers' gloomy predictions were voiced by many of the *Langley* crewmen. Chester and Norman Koepsell were sitting together on the open deck abaft the bridge. As the plane disappeared and the guns ceased firing, Chester said to Norman, "It won't be long now." In fact "it" would be just an hour and forty-five minutes. The delay occurred because the Japanese were at that moment occupied with target practice against a live target.

Just eighty nautical miles east of the *Pecos* four Japanese carriers, the *Kaga, Soryu, Hiryu,* and *Akagi,* steamed in company with their escorts. Included in the attack force were the battleships *Hiei* and *Krishima* and the heavy cruisers *Tone* and *Chikuma.* From the signal yard of an escorting destroyer fluttered the signal "ENEMY TRANSPORT SIGHTED."[26]

On the horizon a small Allied freighter was trying to beat a hasty retreat after having blundered into the powerful Japanese fleet. The carriers, their decks packed with spectators, moved out of the way as the big warships trained their guns on the small, distant target. The freighter was not worth the effort of launching aircraft, but it made an ideal target for a gunnery exercise.

Among the men packed on the *Kaga*'s flight deck was Ensign Shinsaku Yamagawa, a dive-bomber pilot. He was impressed that the ship's batteries fired one gun at a time, "just like firing practice. Really casual." He marveled at how the "water spouts centered virtually in one place and appeared to be one mass." Suddenly the exercise was over. "In a wink it erased the form of the transport from the horizon. It was as though it had never been."

He was cheering with the others when a bugle sounded and the crisp command, "Air crews to the briefing room" was barked over the loud speaker. Full of high spirits and anticipation, Yamagawa ran across the deck closely followed by his squadron leader, Lieutenant Toshio Watanabe.

The briefing was short. A patrol plane had spotted a special service vessel now located approximately eighty miles west of the carrier group and headed south. Four squadrons of Val dive-bombers, one from each carrier, would be launched in sequence. There would be no fighter escort. The mission was considered to be a milk run that would afford the pilots an opportunity to practice their bombing skills in an exercise similar to what the battleships and cruisers had just enjoyed.

Eighty miles away, the *Pecos* was still plodding toward Australia, a goal that Commander Abernethy now seriously doubted he would reach. After the observation plane had flown out of sight, he conferred with his navigator, Lieutenant Francis B. McCall, and Commander McConnell about what to do next. As a result of that conference, the *Pecos* made a radical course change at 1040, turning away from where the Japanese fleet was estimated to be. Thirty minutes later the tanker swung back to within 10 degrees of her original course.[27]

For the next forty-five minutes the *Pecos* headed due south, plowing through a choppy sea. In the charthouse Lieutenant McCall had just put together a table of projected half-hourly dead-reckoning positions, and was reading them to Quartermaster Berry. Berry was carefully recording the figures for use by the radio-room force should the ship be attacked.[28]

On the bridge anxious lookouts strained to spot the enemy they all expected, the strong feeling of danger reinforced by the frequently repeated warning to keep a sharp lookout. The warning had just been given when Coxswain J. Balitzki looked up, shielding his eyes against the sun's glare. There was no specific, conscious thought accompanying Balitzki's looking up. It was simply a gesture made in response to the warning. He did not expect to see the dive-bomber that at that moment was plunging down toward the tanker—but he did.

"Here they come!" Balitzki shouted.[29]

CHAPTER 8

The Attack on the *Pecos*

Despite all the precautions, the extra lookouts, and the repeated warnings to keep a sharp lookout, the *Pecos* was taken practically by surprise.[1] There was a chorus of startled shouts as nearly seven hundred stunned men watched the plane and its bomb part company. Someone on the bridge pressed the alarm button, Commander Abernethy shouted to commence firing, and the first bomb exploded in the water along the port side. Throughout the ship was pandemonium as men dove for cover and others ran toward their battle stations.

Half of the tanker's guns were already manned and quickly opened fire, but most of the ship's crew was in the mess hall. At this critical moment crowds of *Langley* survivors blocked passageways and sprawled across the open decks, making it difficult for the *Pecos* crewmen to get to their battle stations. The problem caused by the ship's overcrowded condition was particularly evident to the officers who were in the wardroom when the first bomb exploded.

The explosion sent most of the officers diving to the deck, but the gunnery officer, Lieutenant Carl R. Armbrust, remained on his feet and started toward his battle station on the navigation bridge. To get there he had to force his way through a packed passageway, run forward along the catwalk above the main deck, and into the bridge structure. The total distance was about 175 feet. The passageway was so crowded that he had to "crawl over bodies as far as the galley deck and then ran crouched along the

This is how the *Pecos* may have looked to a Japanese pilot as he swept down to strafe. The 5-inch gun visible on the forecastle is where D. Harper was injured and many others died. The large whaleboat forward of the bridge was the one used to take off the wounded as the ship went down. The two 3-inch guns are clearly visible amidships as is the catwalk that runs between them from the bridge to the break at the poop. The box-like structure forward of the stack is the radio shack. The boat visible on the boat deck and the raft aft of it were used by the men who panicked and abandoned the ship too soon. (National Archives)

catwalk toward the bridge." As he ran, the *Pecos* twisted left and a second bomb exploded in the water to starboard.

The damage control officer, Lieutenant J. B. Cresap, left the wardroom just as the men in the passageway were getting back on their feet and the *Pecos* crewmen were pushing their way through the crowd trying to get to their battle stations. Cresap's battle station was in the nearby mess hall, but "traffic in the passageway was so heavy and confused" that it was several minutes before he reached his station.

Sixteen-thousand feet above the harried tanker, Ensign Yamagawa circled with the rest of his squadron, watching the first two planes complete their diving attacks. Because there was no threat from enemy fighters, the attack was being made one plane at a time, just as it had been done during training. The ensign noted that there "were numerous, scattered clouds of pure white, but weather was ideal for bombing."[2]

Despite the perfect weather and the absence of fighter opposition, Lieutenant Watanabe's squadron was doing poorly. As he watched, Ensign Yamagawa recorded:

> The first plane released its bomb and pulled up sharply. *Pecos* turned to starboard, dragging her long, pure, white wake. Just as the wake seemed to draw an arc, a great pillar of water rose off the ship's port bow. The second plane released its bomb. The ship, turning hard to starboard, knew the form of certain death. But, regrettably, the ship swiftly changed direction and the second plane raised a pillar of water off the starboard bow.

Impressed with Commander Abernethy's ship-handling skill, Yamagawa later said, "But though they were the enemy, it really was something. The ship's captain certainly was skilled and superbly avoided our bombs." He was also impressed with the volume of antiaircraft fire that rose up from the ship, describing it as "fierce." It was now Ensign Yamagawa's turn to dive on the *Pecos*.

The dive-bomber broke away from the circling planes, pulled ahead of the ship, and swung around to line up on the target. The nose dropped down and the ship entered the bomb sight mounted in front of Yamagawa. The young pilot lowered his dive brakes and swung the bomb from its position beneath the fuselage. The Val, shuddering from the turbulence caused by the extended bomb and dive brakes, hurtled down at the ship. Holding the dive until he was down to 1,500 feet, Yamagawa pulled the release and yanked back on the control column. As the nose slowly rose, there was a loud bang from the engine and the airplane lurched violently. He was hit.

At 1203 Yamagawa's 500-pound bomb arced downward and smashed through the main deck near the starboard 3-inch gun. The explosion tore a hole fifteen feet wide in the deck, smashed four large oil tanks, blew away the firemains, steamlines, air service lines and oil lines that ran forward, and killed or wounded several gunners. The boom on the mainmast, blown out of its cradle, slammed into a port-side king post, bending 45 degrees and crushing a *Langley* survivor, William W. Fowlkes.[3]

Gunner's Mate First Class Frank Doyle was running along the catwalk toward the port 3-inch gun (number six) with his gun crew strung out behind him. Suddenly Gunner's Mate Second Class R. Ward on gun number-five shouted, "Doyle! A Nipper!"[4] Doyle leaped to the base of number-six gun just as the first bomb hit about fifty feet aft. The catwalk vanished under the blast that punched a twelve-foot hole in the deck, collapsed the sandbag barrier around the number-six gun, and blew off the training gear. Fragments killed Seaman First Class Victor "Blueboy" Englehart on the number-five gun and wounded the gun captain, "Jughaid" Crider.

The shock wave swept across the deck, slamming into the radio shack and knocking out all the *Pecos*'s radios. Chief Radioman C. L. Engelman had just entered the radio room when the bomb struck. Picking himself up off the deck, he looked forward and saw the surviving gunners covered with oil from the smashed oil tanks.

Frank Wetherbee from the *Langley* had flattened himself on the main deck just before the bomb exploded forty feet forward. When he quit bouncing around and stood up, he found that he was splattered with oil. Looking forward he saw a huge hole in the main deck formed by deck plates that "were punched down into the oil just like a big funnel."[5]

On the bridge Lieutenant McCall had just arrived and relieved Lieutenant Archibald Stone as officer of the deck. Stone, who had come from the USS *Stewart*, requested permission to reorganize

The *Kaga* launched the first attack on the *Pecos*. (U.S. Naval Institute)

the gun crews on the two 3-inch antiaircraft guns. Commander Abernethy granted permission and Stone hurried away.

On the main deck Doyle crawled from beneath the sandbags that had collapsed on him and looked aft. Seeing the twisted catwalk and huge, smoking hole, he knew his entire gun crew had been killed. But he had little time to think about their fate before the sound of the next bomber filled the air around him.

Scrambling up the ladder onto the gun platform, Doyle grabbed a 3-inch round and slapped it into the breech. The block had just slammed shut when he was joined by "Breezy" McNabb from the *Langley*. Together the two men manned the gun, Doyle in the pointer's seat and McNabb pushing the barrel around by hand.

More *Langley* and *Pecos* men were already running to replace the fallen gunners on both guns when Lieutenant Stone left the bridge. By the time he reached the main deck, Ward's number-five gun was again fully manned and firing, and Stone joined Doyle and McNabb on the number-six gun.

Commander Abernethy was receiving reports of battle damage. Communications had been disrupted between the bridge and the radio room, and the *Pecos* was developing a sharp list to port. There were fires in the oil tanks and another one in the boatswain's locker. To correct the list, which was rapidly approaching 15-degrees, the skipper ordered the oil tanks on the port side pumped out. Additionally, he wanted diesel oil transferred from port to starboard and the starboard oil tanks flooded with seawater.

Unable to reach the radio room by telephone, Lieutenant McCall wrote the dead-reckoning position on a slip of paper and gave it to Quartermaster Berry, with orders to take it to the radio shack. Shortly after Berry delivered the message, Radioman Third Class C. H. Albert learned from Radioman Second Class D. L. Smith and Chief Engelman that they were receiving no acknowledgment. It was the first warning that the *Pecos* was off the air. Albert went forward to the bridge, reported the situation to the captain, and then stood by to run messages between the radio room and the bridge.

Hard on the heels of Albert's disquieting report came more bad news. Lieutenant Cresap reported that the oil lines were so badly damaged that the pumps could not take suction, making it impossible to pump out the port tanks. It also was impossible to transfer diesel oil as ordered because the steam line to the diesel pump had been carried away. Seawater was being pumped in on the starboard side, but even there serious problems had developed. Tanks 11 and 13 had both suffered ruptured longitudinal bulkheads that allowed water pumped into them to run over into the port tanks.

While Commander Abernethy digested the grim reports, he continued to maneuver his ship to avoid the falling bombs. The fourth and fifth bombs fell wide of the mark as the captain handled his ship more like a destroyer than a fat-bellied tanker.

On the open main deck the *Langley* survivors were feeling vulnerable and helpless. Though many *Langley* men had pitched in to help carry ammunition or fight fires, others appeared to be in a state of shock. Ensign Emmanuel, who had joined a large group of *Langley* men on the poop deck recalled:

> The situation had taken on the proportions of a nightmare to all of us. We had survived one disaster only to be precipitated into another hopeless situation. Looking around at my companions, I saw several whose glazed eyes revealed that they were in a state of shock. As far as I was concerned that was as good a condition to be in as any, unless you could be roaring drunk.[6]

On the main deck, Wetherbee suddenly realized that he had no life jacket. Someone had grabbed his, and there was not a loose one in sight. After a hurried search he decided that cover was more important than a life jacket and he ran forward to the bridge structure. The battle din was unnerving, and lacking a battle station assignment, Wetherbee simply wanted to be somewhere safe. Reaching the bridge structure, he wormed himself into a densely packed passageway. Describing events several years later he said:

> A chief from the *Pecos* crew came down the weather deck trying to get someone to carry ammunition. I saw him take hold of the shoulders of two or three men and shake them while telling them what he needed, but they were just frozen like statues. I don't think they even understood him and just went back to their original positions when he let go of their shoulders. I was just about as bad, and on top of that I didn't know the ship, where the magazine or guns were located. Finally I got my head working enough to know we would be in worse

shape than we were if the guns had no ammo—so I caught up with the chief and asked where the ammo was and where he wanted it to go. He said the ammo was clear up on the bow end of the ship and they needed .50-caliber ammo on the fantail. I went to the magazine and carried four belts of .50-caliber, two belts on each shoulder. The trip was about three-fourths of the length of the ship. Each time I had to pass the funnel where the first bomb had hit. I knew if I ever lost my footing I would be funneled into the oil tank and there would be no help.

While the *Pecos* twisted and turned to avoid the bombs, the fires were brought quickly under control. CO_2 was pumped into the oil tanks and fire hoses were run forward from the poop deck. As the fires were put out, choking, dense smoke filled the passageways forcing many *Langley* men from cover and out of their apathy. Many who fled the acrid smoke picked up the small arms that Gunner's Mate Third Class Robert Foley had broken out, and began firing at the Japanese.[7] Though rifles and pistols were ineffectual, having something to fight back with was a big morale booster.

There was so much noise that Ensign Emmanuel, who was lying next to Lieutenant Commander Hale, could hardly hear what Hale was telling him. The *Langley*'s air officer was lying on his back watching the Japanese dive-bombers with an experienced eye. A former dive-bomber pilot, Hale was very critical of the Japanese performance.

"Their angle's not steep enough," he shouted. "Look at this one coming. He's practically glide bombing! Two to one he overshoots," he offered.[8]

Emmanuel looked up at the airplane that was dropping like a stone toward the *Pecos* and "tried to dig a shallow hole in the deck." Hale was still carrying on a running commentary when the bomb exploded in the water, one hundred feet away.

The scene on the *Pecos* was characterized by motion and purposeful activity interspersed with clots of huddled survivors and bedlam. Shouting, cursing men fired at the Japanese, while a few, in frustration, threw potatoes at the diving planes. Others heaved and struggled to drag fire hoses along the sloping deck as corpsmen and doctors hurried to help the wounded. Ammunition was passed along a human chain that ran aft from the magazine near the bow to the two 3-inch guns. Other men, their shoulders draped with belts of .50-caliber bullets and carrying steel boxes of .30-caliber ammunition, scurried in every direction, supplying the machine guns.

On the bridge Commander Abernethy heard that the fires were being brought under control and that oil could be pumped from bunker tank 18, on the port side, to bunker tank 17 on the starboard. In the engine room, deep in the ship, Lieutenant R. L. Mayo was also shifting water in an effort to help put the ship back on an even keel.

At 1215 the *Pecos*'s list had been checked and she was showing signs of slowly starting to right, when the sixth Val unloaded. The heavy bomb hit the water off the tanker's port side, and though the explosion was fairly distant, the shock wave sent a shudder through the tanker when it hit the hull. Below the waterline plates buckled, seams split, and more water rushed in.

Despite the new damage, Commander Abernethy had the situation under control, and his ship had not been mortally wounded. She had steam in all boilers and was still making 12 knots. As the last three planes from the *Kaga* dove and missed, the tanker continued toward her goal and slowly the list decreased.

The Aichi D3A1 Val, a two-place, dive bomber with fixed landing gear. It was this type of plane that bombed and sank the *Pecos*. (U.S. Naval Institute)

At 1227 the *Kaga*'s Vals were headed home across the eighty-mile gap of open sea that separated their carrier from the *Pecos*. As a training exercise, their attack had been a dismal failure. Not only had they failed to sink the tanker, but four of their planes had been hit by antiaircraft fire, and one, Yamagawa's, was in serious trouble. Nevertheless, when squadron leader Lieutenant Watanabe landed, he would report that the *Pecos* "was observed to sink after the attack."

"ATTACKED BY BOMBERS SHIP HIT MAYBE SINKING," followed by the dead-reckoning position was the message being sent at 1227. Actually, the *Pecos* was not in danger of sinking at that moment, though the message being pounded out by Smith and Engelman suggested the possibility. There was still no reply. The only Allied ship near the tanker was the *Whipple*, about fifty nautical miles to the northwest and still on course 279 degrees for Cocos Island.[9] The *Whipple* did not reply because she did not receive the message.

While Engelman and Smith were trying unsuccessfully to tell the world about their plight, Commander Abernethy was preparing his ship for the next attack. To more quickly reduce the list, he ordered seawater pumped into tank 15 on the starboard side, while continuing to transfer oil from port to starboard. At the same time, aware of the fire danger posed by 1,400 gallons of gasoline stored in a forward tank, he ordered fire hoses run out and pumped the gasoline over the side.

Commander Abernethy had won the first round. The tanker's engines continued to function normally, pushing the *Pecos* forward at a steady 12 knots, her steering was intact, and the list was gradually decreasing. The huge hole in her deck and the fires were not enough to kill her or even slow her down. But the tanker's wounds were not Abernethy's only concern, he was also thinking about the casualties among his human cargo.

The crew and passengers had been hard hit by the bomb that had exploded on the deck, and by shrapnel from the near miss. Numerous injuries were being cared for throughout the ship by the four doctors and the pharmacists from both the *Langley* and the *Pecos*. In the captain's cabin, Doctor Blackwell had received most of the men who had been wounded by the first hit. There

were several cases of minor shrapnel wounds, and three serious
burn victims. Among those treated for a shrapnel wound was "Jughaid" Crider who, after his wound had been dressed, returned to
the starboard 3-inch gun.[10]

Already, the scene aboard the listing tanker was starting to
look like a replay of scenes aboard the *Langley*. Echoing Doctor
Blackwell's earlier words, Doctor Yon said, "All that was practical
was to treat burns and stop hemorrhage . . ." The situation was
about to become worse.

At 1300 the *Soryu*'s squadron led by Lieutenant Masi Ikeda
launched its attack. Like those from the *Kaga*, Ikeda's planes would
bomb one at a time at three-to four-minute intervals.

The *Pecos*, fully alerted and prepared, was not caught flatfooted this time. From the tanker's decks a hail of fire rose to meet
the dive-bombers. *Langley* men Jones, Onberg, and Snay blazed
away with Springfield rifles. Around them were men with BARs
and Colt 45s pumping round after round at the Japanese planes.
Lewis guns, mounted in threes and fired with a single trigger,
spewed .30-caliber rounds skyward, accompanied by the longer
reaching .50-caliber machine guns. Three-inch shells burst above
the canopy of criss-crossing, arching tracers.

The spectacular fireworks display above the *Pecos*, though more
impressive than effective, was not entirely without results. To a
degree it unnerved some of the *Soryu*'s pilots, causing them to
release their bombs at a higher altitude than they had intended.

The *Soryu*'s planes made the second and most accurate attack on the *Pecos*,
but they could not sink her. (U.S. Naval Institute)

The *Soryu*'s pilots benefited, however, from the damage that had already been inflicted on the *Pecos*, because it greatly reduced the tanker's maneuverability. That plus their generally superior ability overcame the disruption in plan caused by the heavy antiaircraft fire, and made the *Soryu*'s attack the most effective of the four launched against the *Pecos*.

All those factors were apparent when the first *Soryu* plane nosed over. Inhibited by the streams of tracers that raced up at him, the pilot pulled the bomb release several hundred feet too soon. But he was set up squarely on the target, and the *Pecos*, hindered by tons of water inside her hull, and out of trim, responded sluggishly to her helm. As the bow swung left, the bomb passed through the stern of a 40-foot motor launch stowed just forward of the bridge on the starboard side, punched through the main deck, and exploded in the navigator's storeroom. The blast blew a hole in the starboard side of the hull "large enough to drive a one-ton truck through" and started a fire in two storerooms.

The bridge windows shattered into flying shards that slashed the bridge crew. Fireman First Class Roy J. Marchand died instantly, Saxton was knocked off his feet by a heavy blow to his left arm, and Fireman Second Class J. C. Stafford collapsed with a smashed knee. In great pain, but not bleeding badly, Stafford tried to crawl off the bridge. Struggling across the deck through the broken glass, the fireman asked Lieutenant Armbrust to help him off the bridge. The lieutenant, watching the second plane nose over and start his dive, told Stafford to stay where he was until the bombing stopped.

Lieutenant Armbrust's advice to Stafford was sound. Breaking the bombing pattern established by the *Kaga*'s squadron, Lieutenant Ikeda's second plane dove and dropped its bomb so hard on the heels of the first that the shock of the first bomb had hardly past when the second hit.

The second bomb dropped by the *Soryu*'s bombers scored the third hit on the *Pecos*. The bomb streaked down, struck the foremast at the crow's nest, carrying away the radio antenna and part of the mast without exploding. It then penetrated the main deck at about the centerline and exploded inside an oil tank, carrying away the centerline bulkhead. Because the *Pecos* was still listing as a result of the first hit, the oil in the partially filled starboard tanks flowed into the port tank causing the tanker to list heavily again to port.

Erupting through the deck, the explosion tore away service piping and hurled debris against the bridge structure. One piece of jagged metal cut through the top of the bridge structure and plowed through Seaman First Class Ray Schultz, who was manning the starboard .50-caliber machine gun. He died almost immediately from a massive abdominal wound.

Ensign E. J. Crotty, the antiaircraft plotting officer, was hit so hard by the shock wave that he became "mentally deranged." Wandering aimlessly about, he made his way to the navigation bridge where his incoherent shouts and wild actions caused the bridge crew such problems that Commander Abernethy ordered him restrained.[11]

Commander Abernethy's troubles suddenly multiplied at an alarming rate. The list had reached nearly 20 degrees when the helmsman shouted, "Captain, steering control is lost!" Without hesitation the skipper switched to steering aft and ordered full right rudder to avoid the third plane's bomb. The bomb exploded well off to port and Abernethy sent a messenger aft to tell the executive officer, Lieutenant Commander Lawrence J. McPeak, to be prepared to take over steering if necessary. He then asked for a damage report.

The main cargo pump had stopped, there were fires burning below deck in two forward compartments, and the CO_2 lines to those compartments had been destroyed. There was no water forward of the bridge, the firemain having also been smashed. Looking through the shattered bridge windows, while bracing against the increasing slant of the deck, Commander Abernethy saw smoke pouring from the two bomb holes in the forward deck.

"Send your best man to the pump room, and make every effort to restart it," he ordered, knowing that the ship's list could not be corrected without that pump. The "best man" was Machinist's Mate Second Class R. L. Schuler, who quickly left the engine room and headed for the pump room. Within a few minutes came the word, "Main cargo pump operating."[12]

With the pump back in operation, the process of transferring oil from the low side to the high side was restarted. But it soon became apparent that the mining effect of the several near misses and the imbalance caused by the loss of the centerline bulkhead, made this method too slow. At 1315 the order was given to pump the oil directly into the sea.

Coinciding with that order was a spontaneous rush to abandon ship by several of the men packed on the stern. Undoubtedly the ship's heavy list and the three solid hits that caused so much fire and smoke forward convinced many of the *Langley* survivors that the tanker was sinking. Their fear was heightened by the fact that they were, largely, spectators and felt utterly helpless on the strange ship.

Someone among the passengers yelled "Abandon Ship!" and the rush to the boats started. Coxswain Balitzki, the lookout who had shouted the first warning at 1155, was still atop the bridge. From his vantage point he had a clear view aft. In his narrative he described the scene:

> We were listing badly and everyone got excited aft and started to throw life rafts over and lowered our whaleboats in the water. The word "abandon ship" was not passed from the bridge. The captain hollered not to lower the boats and not to abandon ship, but they ignored the order. All that time they were bombing us and we were firing to keep them away from us.

Ensign C. H. Coburn, a passenger from the USS *Marblehead*, watched in dismay as mattresses, life rafts, and two whaleboats were thrown or lowered over the side followed by "nearly a hundred men."

Walter Sinner and his friend James Puskas were standing together on the poop deck when someone else yelled "Abandon ship." All around them men surged for the boats or leaped over the rail.

"Walt, let's go," urged Puskas, who had been caught up in the panic.[13]

"No. No. Let's hang around," Sinner cautioned. He was not quite certain that the word to abandon ship had come from the bridge.

"This is the time to go! Let's go over," insisted Puskas, who was becoming agitated at the thought of being left behind.

Looking around, Sinner saw dozens of men leaving the ship, but he was still not sure of what to do. "I'll tell ya what," he offered, "let's go forward and jump where is's not so high." Men were now going over the rail in a mass exodus, and Puskas had caught the fever. Without waiting for his friend, Puskas joined the mob and vaulted the rail. Sinner never saw him again.

Two other men were having the same argument. Ensign Martin was standing with an officer named Dye who wanted to get off the listing tanker.

"Let's take the wardroom table and push it over the side," suggested Dye. "Then we'll have a way to survive."[14]

"No. I don't think so," said Martin who was skeptical about the merit of Dye's suggestion.

"Why not?" demanded Dye.

"There are guys back there who have been jumping, and they are going to be out there all by themselves. If she goes down—and she is going down, I won't argue that—I want to be with all the others," Martin explained. Dye remained unconvinced, and like Puskas he had caught the fever. The last that Martin ever saw of him was when he and several *Langley* crewmen shoved the wardroom table over the side and jumped in after it.

Meanwhile, on the boat deck, both port and starboard whaleboats were being filled and lowered. Carl Onberg, from the *Langley*, was near the starboard whaleboat when the panic started:

> There was panic on the boat deck. People came boiling up from the mess deck and started climbing into a whaleboat. Several were the *Langley*'s water tenders. The boat was improperly lowered and it spilled. Most crawled back in but the boat was swept into the starboard screw. It looked like a plastic toy being chopped up.

The scene was witnessed by dozens of horrified *Langley* and *Pecos* crewmen. The *Pecos* listed enough to port that her massive, starboard screw was partially out of the water. Turning at seventy-three revolutions per minute, the huge blade pulverized the whaleboat and its occupants.

As the *Pecos* continued on, her guns blazing away at the Japanese bombers overhead, the occupants of the remaining whaleboat, surrounded by swimmers and men clinging to mattresses, were left behind. Suddenly the men must have realized their mistake for they started waving and motioning, trying to get the *Pecos* to come back. The whaleboat rowed after the ship in a desperate, fruitless bid to rejoin her. Commander Abernethy wanted to put about and pick them up, but damaged and under attack, he could only press forward. The men quickly disappeared astern and were never seen again.

In the meantime Lieutenant Cresap had an extra hose coupled to an after fire plug and led forward to the scene of the fire. There were already men trying to smother the flames with blankets and mattresses. Both *Langley* and *Pecos* men, working under the direction of Boatswain Baumker, had pitched in to fight the fire. When the fire hose arrived, a *Langley* survivor, Seaman Second Class Robert Christensen, donned a breathing apparatus and dropped down into the burning hold. Unable to see because of the dense smoke, and completely unfamiliar with the interior layout, Christensen nevertheless dragged the fire hose into the inferno and stayed until the fire was out.[15]

The indefatigable Boatswain Baumker left the fire scene and turned his attention to doing something to help correct the tanker's severe port list. At the time when the *Kaga*'s planes were leaving, Baumker had suggested to Lieutenant Cresap that the port anchor be let go. The suggestion had been rejected then, but when the boatswain raised the idea again, it was immediately accepted. In a few moments the massive steel anchor was let go and plunged into the sea.

A fourth bomb exploded in the water as the *Pecos* evaded another pass, and angry gunfire pursued the climbing plane. Suddenly the port 3-inch gun ceased firing, a round jammed in its breech. Doyle sent a man forward to the 5-inch guns to get the section staff. Screwed together, the sections would form a long rod that could be inserted down the barrel and placed against the nose of the round. A heavy hammer would then be used to drive the rod against the round and force it back out through the open breech. As designed, the round would not he armed until it had been fired through the gun barrel, and therefore beating on the nose of the unfired round was supposed to be relatively safe. It was the "relatively safe" part that discouraged most people from putting it to the test.[16]

Chief Gunner's Mate F. L. Timmons joined Doyle and Stone at the gun.

"What the hell are you doin, Doyle?" The chief demanded.

"A round is stuck in the damn barrel, and I'm gonna back it outta there," answered Doyle as he screwed the staff sections together.

"Go ahead," roared the chief over the battle noise, "we might as well blow ourselves up as let the Japs do it!"

The staff, rammed down the depressed barrel, was struck on the end with a heavy mallet, dislodging the obstinate round. Even before the defective round splashed into the water, gun number-six was firing again.

Of the four carrier squadrons sent to attack the *Pecos*, Lieutenant Ikeda's nine planes from the *Soryu* were undoubtedly the best. It was a mark of Commander Abernethy's skill and determination that he avoided their bombs as well as he did. His accomplishment is particularly remarkable in view of the damage already suffered by his ship. A fair share of the credit must, however, go to the men who blazed away at the Japanese.

At 1313 the seventh plane started its dive. Engine howling, dive brakes extended, the Val swooped down. The bomb rack swung down and forward, extending its 550 pound load clear of the propeller arc. Fifty-caliber bullets slashed the fuselage and wings as the pilot concentrated on the constantly changing target . At 1300 feet the bomb fell free from the plane and plunged downward toward the tanker's bow.

The bomb smashed through the forward edge of a machine-gun platform and exploded on the forecastle between two 5-inch guns. Both gun crews were wiped out, the dead, the dying, and the wounded scattered on the forecastle deck. The upward blast took out the men on the machine-gun platform, while the downward force tore through the deck, starting fires in the crew compartments and the forward magazine.

Seaman Second Class D. Harper had been a pointer on the number-one 5-inch gun. Just before the bomb hit, Coxswain K. F.

Seaman Second Class D. Harper, the pointer on the *Pecos*'s number-one 5-inch gun. The bomb that hit between the guns killed nearly everyone around him, and left Harper burned and blinded. Despite his wounds he survived. (Photo courtesy of D. Harper)

Grass had shouted, "Take cover!" and Harper hit the deck behind the anchor windlass.[17] Grass's warning had saved Harper's life, but the coxswain died in the explosion. Harper felt a searing heat as the deck buckled beneath him and a wave of hot air rushed over him. His clothes were blown off, his body was painfully burned, and he was momentarily blinded.

Even before the plane pulled out of its dive, men were climbing up on the platform to replace the fallen machine gunners. Reginald Mills and Gunner's Mate Second Class Robert Boswell from the *Langley* were the first to reach the guns. They were closely followed by Howard Whan, also from the *Langley*, until someone shouted, "Don't go up there, they're shooting at you!" The urgency in the voice so startled Whan that he immediately wheeled and ran aft.

The *Pecos* was still jumping from the hit on the forecastle when the eighth plane scored a solid hit amidships. The bomb dropped through the gaping hole abaft the number-five 3-inch gun and exploded deep in the tanker's hull. The shock wave buckled bulkheads and blew open the fire room airlock doors causing a flareback that momentarily left the tanker's boilers without fire.

Shrapnel from the explosion pierced a steam line to the whistle, releasing a cloud of white steam. More steel slivers pelted the antiaircraft guns. Lieutenant Stone was hit in the face and "Jughaid" Crider was hit in the arm and legs. The firing solenoid on the port 3-inch gun was destroyed. Jerking the useless lanyard, Lieutenant Stone swore, "Goddamn gun won't fire!"[18]

Without hesitation he reached under the gun and tripped the sear by hand. As the gun fired, the breech jerked rearward, slamming into Stone's kapok life jacket and knocking him off the platform onto the deck. Quickly climbing back up to the gun the young officer commented, "Ok. We can still fire it."

The blast had shaken the radio shack like a dish rag. The radio room crew continued to send messages while trying to repair damaged equipment and restring fallen antennas. Frequencies had already been shifted four times in an attempt to find someone who would acknowledge that they had been heard. In fact, the *Whipple* may have grabbed a piece of one of those off-frequency transmissions, though she did not answer. At 1324, just as the fourth bomb exploded, the destroyer changed course to 180 degrees true—she was now steaming almost parallel with the *Pecos* and going in the same direction.[19]

In the sick bay Doctor Yon was in the middle of an operation when the bomb exploded. The force of the blast tore the operating table loose and sent it crashing against a bulkhead, bowling over the doctor and his pharmacist assistant at the same time. Tile chips and surgical instruments were hurled across the room and scattered all across the deck. In a memorable understatement Doctor Yon later commented, "Under those conditions it was impossible to work at the operating table."[20]

The patient was laid out on the deck, the pharmacist's mate kneeling beside him to hold him steady while the doctor continued to operate. With one ear cocked for the sound of diving planes and an increase in the tempo of machine-gun fire, the two medical men carried on under nearly impossible conditions. At about the time they expected another bomb to hit, both men dropped to the deck next to the patient and waited for the ship to "stop shudder-ing."

High above the *Pecos* the three remaining Japanese planes circled, watching smoke and steam rise from the listing ship. It was evident to the pilots that the tanker was not sinking—in fact, she had not even been slowed down. But the ship was obviously in bad shape, and the ninth pilot was determined to finish her off.

As the Val hurtled down at the ship, Commander Abernethy swung the *Pecos* to the right in a desperate attempt to evade. Heavy machine-gun and small-arms fire streaked up from the tanker. The target was slowly slipping out of the ring sight mounted in front of the pilot, who was still too high to release the bomb. Watching intently as his plane rushed down at the ship, the pilot could see that it was going to be close.

At 1330 the 500-pound bomb dropped clear of the plane and shot downward. Nearly everyone in the open hit the deck as the bomb plunged into the water right alongside the *Peco*'s port quarter. An enormous tower of water rose straight up beside the ship as the shock wave pounded the ship's hull.

All the gun crews along the port side of the poop deck were wiped out. In the fire room the brickwork in number-three boiler collapsed with a roar and the number-two blower froze in its bear-ings. Simultaneously the fire in number-three boiler was snuffed out and the boiler lost steam. The *Pecos* shuddered, seemed to stumble, and then staggered forward at $10\frac{1}{2}$ knots.

In the fire room, Machinist Louis Czado demonstrated the skill and leadership that earned him two commendations. Describing the machinist's actions Commander Abernethy wrote in his report:

> This officer was in the engine room with regular means of ingress to . . . the fire room blocked by bomb damage. He made his way to the fire room through the washroom and escape trunks, and took charge.

In the smashed fire room Czado secured the boiler, preventing fire and flareback. He then restarted the frozen blower, restoring air pressure in the fire room.

Damage reports came into the bridge from throughout the ship. The fire room had only two boilers operating, reducing the maximum speed to $10\frac{1}{2}$ knots. Also there were several fires forward, but they were being controlled, and several hull plates had been damaged by the mining effect of the near misses. But the pumps were keeping up with the flooding.

At 1335 the last Val headed back toward the *Soryu*, and the sky was clear of enemy aircraft. Smoke rose from the tanker as damage control parties poured water and CO_2 onto the fires. A steady stream of wounded walked or were carried to one of the two dressing stations, while Doctors Handley and Holly moved among those still lying on the deck. The ship's list was slowly being righted and the damage, though heavy, was still not fatal. Commander Abernethy had won round two, but he was already having serious doubts about the outcome of round three.

The *Pecos* enjoyed a lull of about an hour before the next Japanese attackers arrived. Due to a mix-up, the *Hiryu* had launched her squadron late, just ahead of the nine planes from the *Akagi*. Commander Abernethy used the time to tend his wounded, make repairs, and prepare for the near certainty that they were going to have to abandon ship in the near future.

As the last *Soryu* plane flew off, the word was passed for all hands not manning the guns or fighting fires to carry to the weather deck everything they could find that would float. There it would be ready to throw over the side when the time came to abandon ship. Soon the deck was littered with a variety of boxes, table tops, mattresses, and assorted timber.

Doctor Yon received word to move his patients to the starboard quarter deck. As he was directing the move, he heard the word passed for a corpsman to report to the bridge. Yon and Chief Pharmacist's Mate D. Ashcroft continued to work with the wounded until a second, more urgent, call for a corpsman on the bridge was heard. Grabbing a first aid kit, the doctor left the wounded in the care of the *Langley*'s pharmacist, and ran to the bridge.

Arriving on the bridge Doctor Yon saw several wounded men. Marchand was obviously dead, but he had him carried below to Doctor Blackwell's dressing station. He bandaged Stafford's wounded knee, sent him below and turned to the blood-covered Ensign Crotty, who was lying on the deck. Finding no injuries he had the ensign helped below to Doctor Blackwell. The last man treated was Saxton, who still refused to leave his post.

The third attack was launched from the *Hiryu*, whose planes were late arriving over the target. (U.S. Naval Institute)

The list had been reduced to 10 degrees by 1415 and Commander Abernethy wanted to boost the *Pecos*'s speed. The engineering officer, Lieutenant Mayo, told the captain that with only two boilers and a mass of broken lines, there was not enough steam to reach maximum speed unless the steam pump in tank 18 was shut down. Doing that would mean that the list would remain at 10 degrees and might get worse. Eighty thousand gallons of oil had already been pumped over the side, but there were about 20,000 gallons still remaining in the tank. The captain went for speed and at 1415 the steam pump was shut down.

In the radio shack, the *Pecos*'s radiomen had been joined by Charles Snay from the *Langley*. Increasingly concerned by the absence of any acknowledgment to their messages, Commander Abernethy had ordered Snay to see what he could do to help. The decision was fortunate. Snay had been shooting at the dive-bombers with a rifle when he got the word to report to the radio room. When he entered the radio room he saw that "a transmitter had been knocked off its base, and was leaning back on the bulkhead."[21] Inspection disclosed that there was a damaged power cable, a power amplifier tube was not working, and the antenna was down.

It took Snay nearly an hour to repair the damage and "fire off" the transmitter. While two sailors braced the 500-pound transmitter to keep it from "walking off the foundation as a result of vibrations from bomb hits," Snay started sending an off-frequency call for help. Between 1414 and 1428 his broken, slightly off-frequency message was copied by the *Whipple*.

"NERK V NIFQ BOMBED MAY BE SINKING LAT 15 LONG 106" This may or may not have been the first message received by the destroyer, but it was the first message that told the *Whipple* how grave the situation was. In his official report, Commander Crouch described the outcome of a conference he had with the *Whipple*'s captain about the message:

> It was decided that the *Whipple* could arrive at the point of sinking soon after dark and the commanding officer was directed to proceed toward this point.

The calculation about arriving after dark had less to do with distance than it did with simple prudence. The *Whipple* did not

The *Akagi*'s planes finally sank the oiler, but it was a matter of cumulative damage that put her down rather than a demonstration of bombing accuracy. (U.S. Naval Institute)

want to walk into a hornet's nest in broad daylight. At 1430 the *Whipple* was still steaming on course 180 degrees true, making 16 knots. She was about seventy nautical miles northwest of the *Pecos* when the message was received. For the next sixty minutes she steamed on a course nearly parallel to the *Pecos* and slowly began to catch up to the tanker. To the east the *Pecos* pushed her speed back up to 12 knots. The message, "may be sinking," implied some doubt—the doubt would last exactly sixty minutes.

At 1445 the nine-plane squadron led by Lieutenant Takehiko Chihaya from the *Akagi* arrived over the *Pecos*. According to the plan they should have been the last squadron over the target, but the foul-up aboard the *Hiryu* had turned the plan around. Lieutenant Chihaya put his planes in a holding pattern and waited for the *Hiryu*'s squadron to arrive. At 1450 Lieutenant Ichiro Shimoda led his nine planes in and launched the final attack.

Dispensing with the carefully spaced individual attacks that had been used by the first two waves, Lieutenant Shimoda's planes pounced on the *Pecos* in a series of attacks so closely spaced that they seemed to have come all at once. In rapid succession the nine planes dove on the frantically maneuvering tanker raising geysers of seawater all around her but scoring no hits. Two very near misses along the starboard side ruptured the hull and sprayed the bridge with shrapnel, wounding several men. The shocks of those near misses knocked the *Pecos* off the air again.

By now the *Pecos* gunners were largely volunteer replacements who had stepped forward when he original gunners went down. Despite their inexperience, their determination was recorded on seven of Lieutenant Shimoda's nine Vals. Surprised at the ferocity of the antiaircraft fire, most of Lieutenant Chihaya's pilots chose to release at an even higher altitude than had the first three squadrons.

At 1500 they started their attack, coming at the *Pecos* almost one atop the other. Commander Abernethy recalled that as the Vals dove:

> I knew that the ship was doomed. I authorized the communications officer to open up on the radio distress frequency and any other frequency available, and request help. . . . Our position was broadcast, knowing that the Japanese, having tracked us since 1000, already were well aware of our exact position.[22]

Certainly the skipper saw little hope of saving his ship. Badly damaged, holed below the waterline, and listing, there was not much life left in the old girl. But still her gunners had rattled the Japanese, and with any kind of luck the *Akagi*'s planes might all miss, and what would happen after that was anybody's guess. But at 1501 the *Pecos*'s luck ran out. Seven of the nine bombs missed the mark by a wide margin. But pilots seven and eight, showing greater determination than their squadron mates, bore in through the storm of machine-gun fire and released at 1,400 feet.

The seventh pilot dropped his bomb in the water close to the partially exposed starboard screw. The explosion blew men off the fantail and wiped out most of the guns along that side. Marvin Snyder watched one Lewis gunner rise into the air, somersault backwards and fall heavily onto a pile of men huddled on the main deck. As the seventh plane pulled out of its dive, the eighth plane had already released the bomb that finished the *Pecos*. The bomb hit the water near the bow on the port side, caving in the hull below the waterline. Tons of seawater poured in, and the *Pecos* immediately started going down at the bow.

The shock wave from the double blows threw out the breaker on the generator switchboard, plunging the lower decks into blackness. Machinist's Mate First Class D. W. Sego quickly found the trouble and restored the lights. In the engine room, the blast dislodged a pin in the connecting arm to the reversing engine and jolted the lever into reverse. Chief Machinist's Mate W. Harmon crawled between two cylinders and shifted the levers back to the correct position by hand.

On the poop deck the survivors were dragging the dead and wounded away while others manned those machine guns that were still working. Suddenly a sailor appeared on the deck with a white flag tied to a pole. He was attempting to raise the flag when Frank Wetherbee and several other sailors leaped on him. Frank later said, "The nearest three or four men all hit him at the same time and that took care of that."

The *Pecos* was starting to settle faster as the Japanese regrouped overhead. Four of Lieutenant Chihaya's planes had been hit and started back toward the carrier. The rest circled and watched. In the radio room Snay and Engelman were pounding out their calls for help. There had still not been any acknowledgment, and Snay could not tell if his efforts had been successful or not.

On the bridge, Commander Abernethy was listening to Lieutenant Armbrust, who had just returned from having made an inspection of the damage forward. Armbrust reported that under the forecastle the water had risen to within one foot of the main deck, and the magazine was flooded on the port side. There were some small fires below decks abaft the magazine but not much water, though there was ample evidence of flooding. The gunnery officer told the captain that in his opinion the *Pecos* was finished.[23] Even as they stood talking, the tanker listed more heavily to port and the bow sank deeper. At 1530, three hours and forty minutes after the start of the first attack, Commander Abernethy ordered the *Pecos* abandoned.

CHAPTER 9

The *Pecos* Abandoned

"CQ CQ DE NIFQ PLEASE COME LAT 1430 LONG 10630 AND PICK UP SURVIVORS OF PECOS AND LANGLEY CQ CQ DE NIFQ."[1] Without certain knowledge that they were being heard, the *Pecos* radiomen and Charles Snay pounded out the plea for help. Seventy nautical miles east of the *Pecos*'s position a radio operator in the *Whipple* was tuning across several frequencies trying to pick up the faint signal. At 1530 he locked onto the off-frequency transmission and at 1531 the destroyer turned to the left and increased her speed to 19 knots.[2]

Meanwhile the word to abandon ship flashed through the *Pecos*. Lieutenant McCall notified Lieutenant Mayo in the engine room to get his people out, and then with Quartermaster Berry went below to the charthouse for charts and instruments. In the engine and fire rooms the crewmen reacted quickly to the abandon-ship order. The sounds of battle, the heavy list, and the quickening pace as the bow settled left them in no doubt that getting to the main deck had to be done quickly. The fires beneath the remaining two boilers were extinguished, steam valves were popped, and engines were set at stop. Even as these things were being done, men were scrambling up the ladder, through an escape hatch, and onto the port quarter deck. The last men out were Boilermaker Second Class K. W. Bruce and his friend Fireman First Class C. B. Green. After the last man had gone, Lieutenant Mayo made a sweep through the spaces to be sure they were clear before climbing to the main deck. The time was 1535.

The sea around the *Pecos* was already dotted with splashing swimmers, struggling away from the ship through oil-covered water. Chairs, tables, gratings—anything that would float—were being thrown over the side. The badly wounded were being lashed to kapok-filled officers' mattresses and lowered to the water. The decks were crowded with men, some hesitant to leave, others making last minute preparations before going into the water.

David Jones and Walter Kownacki joined a large group of men who were raiding the mess hall for something to eat. Jones recalled:

> We had missed our chance of the second meal that day, and no idea when the next one would be available. Some of us decided to see what we could find before we left, but all we could make use of was a gallon can of pie cherries—not something you want just before a long swim.

Others, with possibly more practical purpose, went in search of water. In a few cases the water came to them. Richard Shanley was standing with a group near the galley passageway when a *Pecos* steward came along with a 3-gallon bucket of water.

"Here. You better take a drink of this. It may be your last one for quite a while," the man said, setting the bucket down on the deck.[3]

Some filled canteens while others simply scooped out a last drink with their hands before going over the side. Harry Mayfield and a few others went further. Harry filled a canteen, armed himself with a .45 Colt pistol, and gave his cash to his friend Seaman First Class Allen M. Hoey, who put it with his money in a condom. Ensign Jay Martin also thought about keeping his money safe, if not dry—he carefully dropped his wallet into the ship's post box.

LONG 10630 PICK UP SURVIVORS CQ CQ DE NIFQ SENDING BLIND SENDING BLIND CASNAY RAD US NAVY SENDING CQ CQ DE NIFQ COM LAT 1430 LONG 10630 PICK SURVIVORS OF LANGLEY AND PECOS CQ CQ DE NIFQ . . . SINKING RAPIDLY AND THE JAPS ARE COMING BACK TO GIVE US ANOTHER DOSE OF WHAT THE US IS GOING TO GIVE BACK IN LARGE QUANTITIES

The message sent at 1538 was the last complete message received by the *Whipple*.

By now the *Pecos* was settling quickly by the bow. Water flowed over the main deck forward of the bridge and the forecastle was awash. The port rail was under to a point forward of the poop deck and the stern was starting to rise. Many men were simply stepping into the water on the low side while others leaped from the higher, starboard rail. As the ship settled, those who were hesitant to leave retreated to the poop deck.

On the port side of the main deck just forward of the bridge structure was a 40-foot motor whaleboat on skids, already partially filled with seriously wounded men. As the ship started down, Doctors Yon and Blackwell, assisted by other officers and men, were trying to heave the boat off its skids. They were soon joined by Lieutenant McCall, who passed his navigation charts and instru-

Pecos officers: 1. Lieutenant (jg) L. O. Davis, supply officer; 2. Lieutenant J. B. Cresap, first lieutenant; 3. believed to be Lieutenant F. B. McCall, navigator. (Photo courtesy of Carl Armbrust)

ments aboard. As water swirled across the deck, the boat floated free and the men climbed aboard.

It was now discovered that the boat's engine was dismantled and there were no oars aboard. Boards floating nearby were fished from the water and used to paddle the boat clear of the ship. While the doctors arranged everyone in the boat, Lieutenants McCall and Cresap pulled three more enlisted men aboard.

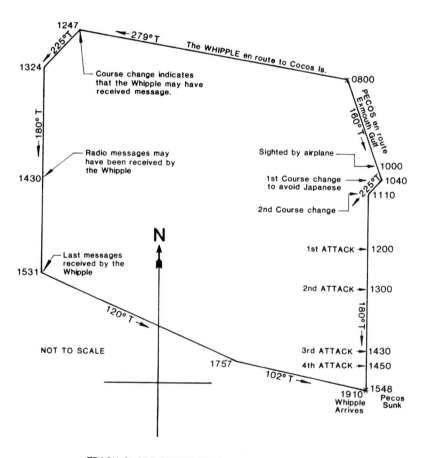

1247
225°T
◄ 279°T
The WHIPPLE en route to Cocos Is.
1324
Course change indicates
that the Whipple may have
received message.
★ 0800
180°T
PECOS en route
Exmouth Gulf
160°T
Radio messages may
have been received by
the Whipple
Sighted by airplane
1430
1st Course change
to avoid Japanese
225°T
1000
1040
1110
2nd Course change
N
1st ATTACK ◄ 1200
Last messages
received by the
Whipple
1531
2nd ATTACK ◄ 1300
120°T
180°T
NOT TO SCALE
3rd ATTACK ◄ 1430
1757
4th ATTACK ◄ 1450
102°T ►
1548
1910 ★ Pecos
Whipple   Sunk
Arrives

TRACK CHART SHOWS THAT WHIPPLE MAY HAVE
PICKED UP AT LEAST A PIECE OF A PECOS
TRANSMISSION BETWEEN 1247 AND 1531

Approximate track chart for the *Pecos* and the *Whipple*, 0800–1910, 1 March 1942.

The entire deck forward of the bridge was now under, and the stern had risen so that the starboard propeller was clear out of the water. From the crowded poop deck men were jumping or sliding down lines and fire hoses to the oily water. At 1340 Charles Snay and Chief Engelman were still in the radio room pounding out the ship's position. Snay recalls:

> I left the door open so that I could gauge the amount of water being taken aboard, and wouldn't get trapped if the ship settled or capsized.

It was a good thing that Snay kept the door open. Two minutes later the operator in the *Whipple* copied a transmission that was "not intelligible, just a dot or dash occasionally." Two minutes later the *Whipple*'s operator copied only "CQ CQ DE NIFQ COME." It was the last transmission from the dying tanker.

On the poop deck, Chief Vano was again reluctant to go into the water. The chief once again did not trust his life jacket and was refusing to go over the side. Finally someone gave him a mattress and pointed out a mess table that would provide the chief with something to float on. Just a short distance away Earl Snyder was again breaking off his cast before going off the ship. Having anticipated the need to shed the heavy plaster, Snyder had been soaking the cast at every opportunity for the past two hours. It now came apart in big soggy chunks. By the time he had the cast off he was so weak from shock and the effects of morphine that he collapsed on the deck.

Vano was still trying to make up his mind when a *Pecos* corpsman grabbed the mattress from him and started lashing the helpless Snyder to it. While Snyder was being lowered to the water, Vano decided to jump for the mess table. Only half convinced that he was doing the right thing, the chief leaped away from the ship and fell twenty feet to the water. When he surfaced the mess table was gone.[4]

As the stern rose higher and the deck grew steeper, many men were paralyzed with fear and clung desperately to whatever they could find, while others clambered over the stern or jumped from the rail. Akerman and Dix, the two Army pilots, were on the starboard poop deck. Dix went over the rail and down a line to the starboard propeller shaft that was now twenty feet out of the water.

He shouted up to Akerman to follow, but Akerman's hand was so badly injured that he could not hang on to the line. The stern was starting to rise quickly and Dix could not wait any longer. Looking up one more time he saw his friend was gone, and Dix jumped.

Sitting on the starboard side of the hull midway between the bridge and the poop deck were Commanders McConnell and Divoll. Both men had taken off their shoes and were easing themselves down the sloping hull. Looking aft and up, Divoll saw the huge starboard propeller turning slowly.

"Jesus! I don't want to be sucked down and I don't want to be cut up by that prop!" he shouted to McConnell. The *Langley*'s skipper looked up and shouted, "Let's go!"[5]

The threat posed by the *Pecos*'s propeller was nothing compared to that which swept down from the sky. The last three Vals peeled off and streaked across the water, machine-gunning the swimmers. As the bullets beat on the water it was quickly apparent that the two or three large groups that had already formed were attracting the pilots' interest. Chester and Norman Koepsell stopped swimming and shouted to those around them to spread out and avoid the crowds.

To Harry Mayfield there was no distinction being made between lone swimmers and groups. He watched a plane bear down on him until it looked like the front view of a recognition silhouette. A solid column of foaming geysers marched across the water directly at him. Mayfield shed his life jacket and thrust himself down as deep as he could go. Around him the sea hissed and foamed as the bullets pounded the water and he could feel the engine vibrations when the plane thundered over. Popping back to the surface, Mayfield took a deep gulp of fresh air and looked for his discarded life jacket. All he found were tattered pieces.

Walter Kownacki also tried to duck beneath the surface as the strafers beat the water with machine-gun fire. But Kownacki forgot to shed his life jacket, and could not push himself under. In desperation he stuck his face in the water, achieving scant security from the ostrich-like maneuver. Luckily for him, he was outside the fire zone.

One of the pilots had still not dropped his bomb before starting the strafing run. As the three Vals swooped down on the struggling swimmers, the one with the bomb brought up the rear. That plane had just started its run when, on the fantail, the *Pecos*'s executive officer, Lieutenant Commander McPeak, grabbed a .50-caliber machine-gun and opened up on the last attacker. Nearby, Ensign Martin manned another machine gun.[6]

The sudden, unexpected burst of fire from the sinking ship caught the last pilot by complete surprise. Tracers from McPeak's gun neatly hemstitched the plane's belly. Chunks of engine cowling and wing were blown off, and white smoke belched from the engine. The startled pilot, realizing that his plane was badly hit, unloaded his bomb three hundred feet astern of the *Pecos* and banked away sharply. McPeak's tracers continued to reach out for the smoking plane that quickly disappeared from sight behind the long swells.

The port bridge wing was awash and the stern was rising in a jerky motion, like an elevator stopping at each floor, when Commander Abernethy stepped off his bridge and into the water. For a terrifying moment he felt himself being dragged down; he struggled toward the surface, while high above him men leaped from the stern that was now nearly sixty feet above the water.[7]

The paralysis that had been evident earlier had now become epidemic. Many men were frozen with fear as the height above the water and the angle on the deck increased. Frank Wetherbee recalls:

> The bow was down and the stern was fifty or sixty feet in the air. To get around without sliding forward you had to hang on to something. There was an officer back there . . . he had just come from below decks. The *Pecos*'s executive officer was trying to get him to get off the ship but he wouldn't do it. He just sat there with a faraway look in his eye and said "I'll stay here,"—and he did. I was behind another guy and I didn't feel we had much time to lose. He wouldn't jump so I told him to get the hell out of the way and let somebody get there who would. He didn't jump but he stepped aside and I jumped.

At 1545 the *Pecos* started her final plunge. Commander Abernethy, his executive officer, and Lieutenant Armbrust had gone into the water only moments earlier. Still close to the hull were Foley, Wetherbee, Ensign Martin, and the radio room crew that

Pecos officers: 1. Boatswain Robert Baumker, assistant first lieutenant; 2. Commander E. Paul Abernethy, commanding officer; 3. Doctor J. L. Yon; 4. Lieutenant Carl Armbrust, gunnery officer; 5. Lieutenant Commander Lawrence McPeak, executive officer. (Photo courtesy of Carl Armbrust)

had left the ship only moments before the captain. Nearly a hundred men still clung to the poop deck.

Richard Shanley and Chief Pharmacist's Mate Harold Spidel had gone off the ship together just as the stern started to rise. Before going over they had collected several mattresses and had lashed them together with marlin line to form a rather substantial and buoyant raft. They had also strapped on their "tin hats" as a protective measure against strafing. Now they found themselves in the water next to the ship as the stern began its rapid ascent prior to the *Pecos* taking her last plunge. Terrified, the men abandoned their carefully prepared mattress raft, shed their helmets, and swam as hard as they could away from the ship.

The tanker's stern rose steadily higher, the hull rotating slowly around its longitudinal axis in a partial pirouette imparted by the heavy port list. From inside the hull came heavy booming noises as machinery and equipment tore loose and crashed through the forward bulkheads.

One hundred and fifty yards away Millard McKinney watched the stern lift "until the ship was vertical." Thomas Spence watched a screw turn slowly as the ship started to slide under, and David

Jones was horrified as the ship's downward momentum increased and he saw "people jumping off the stern onto the screws, into the water." Robert Foley saw "all kinds of things falling off—bodies, debris, all kinds of stuff." The *Pecos* plunged downward and was abruptly gone, her resting spot marked by debris and an outward expanding wave that rolled beneath the oil-covered water. It was 1548.

The immediate reaction among the swimmers was loneliness and despair. Spence said that he felt an "ungodly lonely feeling after the *Pecos* went down," and David Jones noted that "even though she wasn't our ship there was a profound sense of personal loss." The feeling of loneliness and despair was well founded. Every man in the water knew that the Indian Ocean was virtually empty of Allied shipping. None of the men, not even the radio operators, knew if their messages had been received, nor could they say with any certainty that a ship would come looking for them if the messages had been heard. Lastly, they all knew that even if a ship did come, finding them would be very difficult.

The seriousness of their situation was made worse by the condition of the water around them. The sea was very rough and covered with a heavy coat of oil. The oil burned their eyes, blinded some of them, and attacked the sensitive throat and nose tissues. The rough seas broke over them so that they involuntarily swallowed the black, nauseous gunk and became ill. It is little wonder that faced with the small likelihood of rescue, tossed about by the waves, blinded and choked by oil, many simply gave up and sank beneath the waves.

But among most of the swimmers there persisted a powerful will to survive. Groups were already forming, and two of those early collections soon grew to one or two hundred men. The wounded were passed to the center of those large groups and, in some instances, were placed in the large balsa rafts that formed the nucleus. But there were only two or three balsa rafts, and most of the groups—forty to sixty men—were gathered around debris that had been roped together.

Using a wooden sawhorse for extra flotation, Frank Doyle was working his way toward a group when he spotted his friend "Pappy" Lass.

"Pappy! Can I swim with you?" shouted Doyle. "Sure," said Lass and turned toward Doyle.

Doyle was surprised to see that his friend had been hit in the face and appeared badly hurt. Helping Lass onto the sawhorse, Doyle pushed his burden toward a large group. He had not gone far when he came upon Chief Vano who, despite his life jacket, seemed to be having trouble keeping afloat. Doyle shoved a piece of wood to Vano who instead of grabbing the proffered board, grabbed Doyle. The two men thrashed around until Doyle was able to disentangle himself from the frightened chief and get him onto the plank. Vano stopped struggling once he was on the board, and Doyle resumed his pusher duties toward the distant group.

Commander Abernethy had found a wooden locker and made repeated attempts to climb onto it. But the oil-covered surface was so slick that he kept falling off. He finally gave up and joined Commanders McConnell and Divoll, who were trying to lash several bamboo poles together with belts. No matter how hard they tried, they could not keep the poles together.

Charles Snay soon joined them and suggested that they swim to a larger group that was better organized and had more substantial flotation. McConnell and Divoll took the warrant officer's suggestion and headed for the larger group. Snay splashed off to gather in more stragglers, and Abernethy was left alone.[8]

Snay's efforts were typical of those made by several officers and men to keep everyone together and their spirits up. Ensign Ditto swam around his group "like a sheepdog," herding stragglers back and trying to save those who gave up. He entertained the men with jokes and crazy antics in an effort to boost their spirits. Claud Hinds later told the press, "75 to 100 of us were interested for an hour at Ditto's antics as he played with a dead flying fish."[9]

Not everyone was in a large group. Many drifted alone or in pairs, separated from their comrades by the heaving waves. Akerman and Dix had found each other, and hung between two long shoring timbers. Abernethy clung to a piece of flotsam. Walter Sinner and five *Pecos* crewmen had crossed and locked arms across two mattresses. James Saulton and his friend Delbert Pope clung to a large wooden ration box and avoided joining with anyone else, "mostly because we didn't want to share the box." Frank Wetherbee

Second Lieutenant Gerald Dix and his friend William Akerman were the only two Army Air Force men to survive the ordeal. Akerman was killed in 1943, and Dix ended up in a German prison camp. He is shown here in 1954 when he commanded the 366th Fighter Wing. (Photo courtesy of Gerald Dix)

alternately drifted and swam, sometimes looking for a group and sometimes avoiding them.

Wetherbee had been with a half dozen men but had gone off to find something more substantial with which to build a raft. He found what he wanted, a thick couch cushion, but then realized that he had gone "a lot farther" than he thought, and he could not relocate his group. Deciding to find some company, he paddled along on his cushion until he spotted another group.

> I spotted what looked like a large group and I headed that way. They were probably a mile off and when I got closer it was thirty to forty men. They had what I think were big bamboo poles fastened together. The ship had quite a bunch of them which were put over the side. When I was close enough to hear, the men were quarreling among

themselves. It seemed that they could all hang on to the poles all right, but some would try to get on top and ride and then the poles would sink. The last thing I heard was when one told the other, "I have told you for the last time; next time I am going to slit your so and so throat from ear to ear." I decided I wouldn't be any better off with that company and went right on by.

Whether in groups or in pairs, there were two subjects about which the men talked—the possibility of rescue and the possibility of sharks. Despite a rumor that a ship was coming back for them, most of the men did not think they had much of a chance to survive. The pessimism was so strong that several simply said, "The hell with it," shed their life jackets, and sank.

The shark threat fortunately did not materialize and while it caused a lot of anxiety, it provided one of the few light moments. Several men had armed themselves with .45-caliber pistols or bayonets before abandoning ship, with the idea that the weapons might be useful against sharks. Not long after they entered the water, the problem those heavy objects caused outweighed any usefulness they might have had against sharks, and they were discarded.

Carl Onberg was clinging to the periphery of a very large group when a wave tore him loose and swept him away. Alone, Onberg shed his extra gear, including a pistol, and started to swim toward another group. Just as he approached the mass of men and debris, something rough brushed his bare foot. Onberg "knew" his foot had been brushed by a prowling shark and he jerked his feet up beneath him, grabbing both knees with his hands. A thousand ill-defined visions rushed through his mind as he floated in a sort of "cannon ball" position staring tensely ahead, afraid to look down or around. Nothing happened. Onberg held his tightly balled position for a long time, until he slowly overcame his initial panic. Finally he relaxed, lowered his feet, and looked around. Floating within an arm's length, just beneath the surface was a partially waterlogged mattress.

Onberg's experience of being torn away from the edge of a group was a common one and accounted, in part, for the enormous number of men who drifted alone. James Harvey said:

> There were three or four groups. They started with someone clinging to some sort of flotation. Usually it was tables, fenders and poles, but

in one or two cases they had a big balsa raft. Others joined them and added more flotation that was somehow lashed together. The wounded usually ended up in the center and everyone else hung on to the guy in front of him so that pretty soon there was a big ring of people around the central debris. There was a constant sluffing off at the group's fringe. Some who were torn away swam back, but others just drifted away.

Some men left their groups on purpose, usually because they believed that their chances for survival would be better somewhere else. Typically, the movement was from small groups to large, as was the case when Howard Whan left his group.

Whan was clinging to a pole with six men as darkness started to fall. The seven had been arguing about their chances for survival and finally Whan said, "Look, there isn't any way in God's world you're gonna get picked up if you don't join a big group. They ain't gonna pick up a few stragglers!"

"You do what you want," members of the group told him, "we're staying with the pole."

Whan pushed away from the pole and swam toward Ensign Ditto's group. Twenty minutes later he was hanging on at the edge of the much larger cluster of survivors. He never again saw the men who stayed with the pole.

Lester Bates left his group for peace of mind. He had been part of a fairly large cluster around one of the balsa rafts but had become "disgusted" when one of the men started singing religious songs. Bates, who described himself as nonreligious, figured it would take more than singing to save them and set out to find a quieter group. He soon joined Bernard Jasper and his companions who were clinging to several cane fenders. As far as Bates knows, no one who was on the raft he left survived.

By nightfall, more men were resorting to prayer as the best means to speed rescue. In fact, there was little else they could do but drift, hope, and pray. Tragically, the number who gave up and let themselves drown also rose.

At about sundown an event occurred that few could accurately identify but about which many accurately guessed. Commander Abernethy recorded in his official report, "About 1800 . . . heard explosions toward the northeast as if some ship were being bombed."

The *Edsall* was lost with all hands on 1 March 1942, and the explosion heard and felt by the *Pecos* survivors during the evening may have come from the destroyer's last battle. (National Archives)

Ensign Emmanuel later wrote, "Toward twilight, I heard what seemed to be bomb explosions in the distance. It may have been bombs bursting on the *Edsall*."

In fact, Ensign Emmanuel may have been right. Between 1720 and 1902 the *Edsall* was attacked by cruisers and battleships of Admiral Nagumo's carrier force and aircraft from the *Akagi* and the *Soryu*. Of the *Edsall*'s crew, and thirty-two Army passengers, only eight were fished out of the water by the Japanese. What later became of those eight is unknown.[10] None of the thirty-two P-40s, their pilots, or the ground crews reached Java. The price paid for the mismanaged attempt to reinforce Java's fighter strength was thirty-two fighters, one seaplane tender, a fleet oiler, and a destroyer. The casualties among the ships' crews were as yet undetermined, but the number would be high.

Even as the distant rumbling and the shock waves reached the drifting men, Commander Abernethy noticed that the motor whaleboat containing the doctors and the seriously wounded had disappeared. Lacking mechanical power, oars, or sails, the wind had slowly pushed the boat farther away from the swimming men. Lieutenant McCall had seen the problem at once and knew that their best hope for rescue lay in staying as close to the main group as possible. But drifting was not the only threat to survival faced by the men in the powerless whaleboat.

The boat's rudder had been smashed when the boat floated off the sinking tanker's deck. Without power or means of control, the boat lay in the troughs of the waves, rolling heavily and shipping water. To counter the problem, Lieutenant McCall jury-rigged a small sail in the stern and streamed a homemade sea anchor from the bow. It was hoped that the sail would cause the boat to round-up into the wind and that the sea anchor would hold the bow there. In fact, the attempt met with only "partial success," but it was enough to reduce the amount of water the boat was taking, and, unknown to McCall, would put the boat directly in the *Whipple*'s path.

As daylight faded so did the few remaining hopes. The sea became rougher, and there was no escape from the nauseating oil. In the dark men cried, moaned, and called for help. Fatigue and exposure made their misery worse. Men who clung to bamboo poles and shoring timbers were chafed raw by the violent pitching motion. All of them were getting tired, and few of the men who were separated from their groups had enough strength to swim back.

Walter Kownacki was clinging to the outside edge of a group of about fifty or sixty men. Their nucleus was a makeshift raft of timbers and table tops on which lay three seriously burned men. Kownacki recalls that as darkness came on "fewer and fewer guys hung on." As they dropped off, he was able to work his way forward until he actually reached the raft. By that time there were not more than a dozen men around the raft. Bates recalls that during the period after nightfall several men around him wanted to drown themselves, and swam away. Bates tried to stop them, but he was too tired to prevent them from going. Soon his group was down to two. David Jones watched several men drown themselves, and the man next to Tom Spence said, "I'm getting the hell out of here!" He swam out a few yards, shed his life jacket and sank. Wetherbee was floating with a young sailor who was holding on to a chair:

> I didn't pay any attention to him for three or four minutes, and when I turned to say something to him the top of his head was all that showed. The life jacket wouldn't let him sink any more and I can still see his reddish-brown hair going up and down in the water.

Tragically, many who gave up did so just as help arrived.

Though the night was dark, visibility toward the horizon was fairly good, which meant that an object that rose above the waves could at least be seen as a dark silhouette. Looking across the heaving black waves a man could see nothing except what was close by. Looking out at the horizon when atop a wave was another matter. At 1910 one of the men in the stern of the whaleboat spotted a dark silhouette coming directly toward them. Doctor Yon seized a flashlight, pointed it toward the ship, and flashed "SOS SOS SOS."

Commander Divoll was staring absently into space when he noticed that the stars were "being successively blacked out." Rising to the top of a wave, he saw the familiar outline of a four-piper. "There's a destroyer!" he yelled.

James Harvey, his vision dimmed by oil, thought he saw masts and shouted, "Hey! Look!" The men around him saw the masts too and started yelling. Though the ship appeared to be about a mile away, Harvey started swimming toward it.

Ensign Emmanuel was floating among a large group that included Boswell, Mealley, Stafford, Saxton, Baumker, and Shanley. Emmanuel had earlier taken a flare gun from an injured *Pecos* quartermaster who was now with the other wounded in the raft at the group's center. Hearing the shouts, he hastily loaded the Very pistol, pointed it overhead, and pulled the trigger. Nothing happened. Shanley swam to Emmanuel, examined the gun, and started taking it apart. Emmanuel held the parts in his hand while Shanley repaired and reassembled the gun. A new flare was shoved into the breech, the barrel snapped shut, and pointed straight up. At 1916 a white flare exploded overhead.[11] The Very star that came from dead ahead was seen at once by the bridge lookouts on the *Whipple*. Out of the night came shouts and dozens of winking lights. More flares streaked skyward, some to starboard, some to port. Boarding ladders, knotted lines, cargo nets, and fire hoses were hurriedly draped down both sides of the *Whipple*. Dozens of sailors lined the rails to help pull the survivors aboard while others stripped off their clothes, ready to dive in after the weak and the injured. At 1722 the *Whipple* "went to general quarters and maneuvered to pick-up survivors."[12] Commander Crouch reported:

> The *Whipple* slowed and commenced recovering survivors. They were widely scattered . . . separated by groups of sixty or seventy on rafts and various driftwood which they had accumulated after the ship had sunk.[13]

For the next two hours and forty-three minutes the *Whipple* circled, stopped, drifted, and circled again. One moment she would be nearly on top of an exhausted swimmer, and then she would move away out of reach. Men who saw her as just an indistinct blur, and who knew they had no hope of reaching her, suddenly found themselves right alongside her hull as a result of a position change. Fate played a heavy hand in determining who was rescued and who was not.

Among those who were rescued early were Akerman and Dix. The two pilots first became aware of the destroyer when men around them began shouting, "Help!" and "Over here!" Both men were

The *Whipple* rescued many of the *Langley* crewmen twice. During the second rescue she was driven off by a Japanese submarine, leaving nearly two-thirds of the swimmers behind. (U.S. Naval Institute)

totally exhausted and did not have the strength to swim toward the destroyer that was just a few yards away and getting closer. Life lines splashed into the water around them and each man grabbed one, but alongside the ship only Akerman was strong enough that he could be hauled aboard unassisted. A swimmer leaped from the destroyer, tied a line around Dix, and strong arms heaved him up the side.

David Jones and Jesse Sellers, the boatswain's mate who, with Ensign Emmanuel, had tenaciously fought the inferno on the *Langley*'s poop deck, were also among the early rescues. Jones "saw a faint light that soon was recognized as a ship drifting backwards through survivors." When the ship was fifty to one hundred feet away, Jones and Sellers swam for it.

Among the first brought aboard were the men in the whaleboat with Doctors Blackwell and Yon. At 1935 they were all aboard and

Pecos officers: 1. Doctor J. L. Yon; 2. Lieutenant J. L. LaCombe, communications officer; 3. Ensign W. J. Crotty, assistant supply officer. (Photo courtesy of Carl Armbrust)

the empty boat was set adrift. Lieutenant McCall went directly to the bridge to help direct the *Whipple* toward the bulk of the swimmers.

As the men in the water watched the *Whipple* move slowly through the area, they were faced with the need to make what literally might be a life or death decision—stay together in groups or strike out, every man for himself, toward the destroyer. The decision to stay with the group or to swim off toward the ship was often a tough choice. There was no universally correct answer; it all depended on the individual circumstances. Those who elected to remain in groups argued that the destroyer's lookouts would spot large groups more easily than individual swimmers. There was also a belief that reflected a comment made earlier by Howard Whan, when he left a small group to join a larger one—the destroyer would not bother with small groups of stragglers but would concentrate on saving the large groups.

Those who wanted to leave their groups and swim for the ship were motivated by the strong belief that the ship would only pickup those men who were alongside. Her maneuvers often appeared to be taking her away from, rather than closer to, their position. Lastly, they were sure that the "tin can" would not spend much time in the area, and waiting to be rescued was wasting precious time.

For many men there was no decision to make—it had effectively been made for some of them. Those were the men who were wounded, too exhausted, or too sick to reach the ship by swimming. Others were simply afraid to leave whatever security was afforded by the debris to which they clung. Collectively, the wounded, tired, and fearful represented about half the men drifting in the oily water. For them there was no choice but to drift, wait, and hope that the destroyer would come to them. For most of them the destroyer never came.

John Kennedy was clinging to a bamboo pole with eighteen dispirited sailors. As the heavy pole rose Kennedy saw the *Whipple* and shouted, "I see a ship out there!"[14]

"Oh, don't tell us that if it isn't true."

"It's true," Kennedy insisted, "I see a ship."

"Is it one of ours or theirs?" asked a weakened sailor.

"How the hell do I know? Whatever it is, it's better than what we've got," replied Kennedy. He recalls the others were in bad shape from oil-caused sickness and fatigue. The destroyer was still about a quarter mile away and seemed to be stopped.

"I'm going to swim over to her," he told the eighteen, but there was no indication that anyone of them would go along.

"Ok, send them back for us," one of the men called back.

"Ok," said Kennedy as he pushed away from the log. He does not recall how long he swam, but it seemed forever. Reaching the *Whipple*'s side, he was thrown heavily against the hull by a large wave and swept astern by the current.

"Hey!" he hollered.

"Here's another one," someone yelled, and a line splashed into the water beside him. As he flopped onto his back, Kennedy told his rescuers "There are eighteen guys out there."

"Where?" asked a *Whipple* crewman. Kennedy stood up, turned to point, but saw only a black heaving sea.

"Where I came from," he stammered.

"We don't know where you came from, buddy." Kennedy was cold and beat. He continued to stare into the black night, only dimly aware of the bustling activity around him as more survivors climbed or were dragged aboard. Finally someone grabbed his shoulders, and a voice said, "Better get below, guy." The eighteen were never found.

The water on both sides of the destroyer was thick with splashing men. Many were too weak to make the hand-over-hand climb up the knotted ropes or pull themselves up the cargo nets. Most wore life jackets, a few did not, and occasionally a swimmer could be seen still wearing his tin hat. Those near the ship gripped the wood belt that banded the ship at the waterline, or clung to the lines and nets. As the ship rolled they would be hoisted out of the water and then dashed beneath the surface.

Panic was starting to develop as more men reached the ship's sides. The boarding process was slow. There was not room for everyone on the cargo nets, nor were there enough lines and fire hoses to handle even the strong men. Swimmers from the *Whipple* were outnumbered thirty or forty to one by the weakened men who needed their help to get aboard.

On Emmanuel's raft the men waited with growing impatience while the *Whipple* maneuvered among the swimmers. After about an hour, the destroyer circled and came closer to the group, but still remained some distance away. A chorus of voices urged that they all make a try for the destroyer.

Ensign Emmanuel spoke against the idea, "The reason it's taking so long for that ship to get over here is because of all the stragglers. So we are going to stay together. No one leaves the raft and we will all be picked up together."[15] The ensign's argument was generally accepted by the nearly one hundred men on the raft.

In the meantime a much smaller group consisting of Shepston, Paul Burroughs, the Koepsell brothers, and Don Brown had joined a large collection led by Ensign Ditto. When the *Whipple* was about 200 yards away, Shepston heard someone yell, "Let's swim for it."

"I'm not the best swimmer," said Burroughs hesitantly. "I think I'll stay with the raft."

"Come on," urged Shepston, anxiously eyeing the destroyer. "We'll help you."

"No! I'm staying here till they pick me up." The four friends were reluctant to leave Burroughs, but they felt it was a matter of now or never. All four made it, but Paul Burroughs was not picked up.

Another small group made up of Harry Mayfield, Allen Hoey, George Fisher, and John Black were drifting away from the *Whipple*. The ship was clearly picking up survivors and moving forward slowly. The four sailors realized that if they waited any longer, they would be left behind.

"It's every man for himself," shouted Mayfield, and the four splashed toward the ship. The going was hard and the four friends were quickly separated. Mayfield and Black got aboard the *Whipple*, but Hoey and Fisher were never seen again.[16]

At about the same time, Lester Bates and another man were struggling toward the *Whipple* when suddenly Bates shouted "She's not stopping, we better swim for it!"

"You go on. I'm too tired." The other man answered weakly.

Bates's life jacket had become so water-logged that it was doing more harm than good, and he slipped out of it. The life jacket sank as Bates swam hard for the *Whipple*. After he had gone about half the distance he realized that he would do better without his shirt on and quickly pulled it off. When he resumed his race toward the *Whipple*, he was nearly naked and several hundred dollars poorer. The money he had scooped up after he had abandoned the *Langley* was in the shirt.

Bates was right when he concluded that the destroyer was not stopping. Lieutenant Commander Karpe was circling to bring his ship back among the heaviest concentration of survivors. In Ensign Emmanuel's group James Mealley watched the destroyer approach them for a second time. Again there were admonishments to stay together as more men announced their intention to swim for it. When the destroyer stopped about fifty yards away, Mealley and about half the group decided it was time to go. Fate was again a major factor in what caused some to live and others to die. About half of Emmanuel's group survived. Curiously, the survivors were evenly divided between those who elected to swim to the destroyer and those who chose to wait with the raft.

The distance—about fifty yards—was short, but for many it was simply too far. An anonymous *Pecos* survivor later wrote:

> There is something terrible about seeing a man swim valiantly along, trying hard to remain above the water, trying to go on living, imbued with the will to live, and then see him reach for a stroke, miss, and slide slowly under. There is no sound more eerie than the call of a man for help when you are powerless to aid him.[17]

But not all of those who reached the ship were saved. There are numerous cases in which two friends, after reaching the destroyer, waited together for an opportunity to climb aboard, but on the following day one found the other was missing. Some were swept past the ship, others were overcome by exhaustion or wounds at the last minute. At least one man was killed when the ship pitched and the stem smashed his skull.[18]

Though it was generally the case that the strong survived, there were strong men who did not, and many died trying to save the weak. Robert J. Baumker, the boatswain from the *Pecos*, was among them. He was the man who had executed the open sea transfer with such commensurate skill, and who had energetically led the tanker's forward damage control party. He had continued to be a leader as the *Pecos* went down, launching a life raft and seeing that the wounded were placed in it. Throughout the long hours in the water he had gathered more men around the raft and had tirelessly gone after those who drifted away. As the raft bumped against the destroyer's hull he remained in the water assisting the wounded and the weak aboard.

Another strong man who was not picked up was Machinist Butts. Snay recalled that "he could easily hold me over his head." Like Baumker, Butts had been a tower of strength and encouragement to the men around him during the long hours in the water. He too put others ahead of himself using his strength to help men aboard who were too weak to make it themselves. Butts and Baumker were still in the water alongside the *Whipple* at 2141 when the ship got under way.

"Submarine contact bearing 130 degrees true." Rescue operations ended abruptly as the destroyer quickly worked up to 15 knots and started to maneuver, looking for the submarine. The men clustered along both sides of her hull were left spinning and tumbling in the churned up wake and tossing waves. At 2148 the *Whipple* dropped two depth charges. Powerful shock waves raced out from the explosions' centers, intended to smash the submarine pressure hull. Instead they smashed men.

There was, of course, no alternative. The destroyer had to get under way and she had to attack the submarine. To have done otherwise would have resulted in the loss of the ship and increased the number lost. Nevertheless, it was a painful decision for Lieutenant Commander Karpe, but not nearly so painful as the one he would have to make seven minutes later.

At 1252 the *Whipple* slowed to bare steerage and resumed rescuing survivors. The men who were picked up during the next four minutes may be among the luckiest people on earth. The cargo nets were still draped down the destroyer's hull as were some of the knotted lines forward. Reginald Mills was too tired to swim any more, but suddenly the ship was coming directly toward him. As she crept past he grabbed the cargo net, and using the last of his strength, pulled himself up to the deck.

Other men grabbed lines and netting. Those too weak to hang on fell back into the sea, others like Earl Snyder entwined themselves in the cargo net and dangled there until helping hands from the deck hauled them aboard. Probably not more than ten or fifteen people were rescued during the four minutes between 2152 and 2156. The last man aboard may have been Charles Snay, the radioman whose off-frequency transmissions had brought the *Whipple* back.

Snay had been alongside when the *Whipple* had first heard the submarine. He and the *Langley*'s navigator, Lieutenant Commander Soule, were waiting at the outer edge of the mass of men waiting to climb aboard, when the destroyer suddenly lunged forward and charged away. Like Mills, Snay and Soule were nearly done in with fatigue and nausea when the *Whipple* unexpectedly turned back toward them and slowed.

It looked to Snay as though she was barely moving as he and Soule used the last of their strength to swim toward the destroyer. As he reached the ship, Snay recounts:

> I pushed the navigator to the starboard side where a cargo net was strung and made sure he was out of the water. I had to clear the side or get caught in the prop, . . . caught the sea ladder on the starboard side and climbed aboard.

About the time that Snay was clutching for the sea ladder, another submarine contact was made and propellers were heard dead ahead, less than 200 yards distant. The *Whipple* again charged into the darkness, dropping two more depth charges at 2158. For seven minutes the destroyer searched for the submarine while the officers from all three ships discussed what to do next. At 2205 the *Whipple* "abandoned the rescue of survivors due to submarine danger" and cleared the area.

She had picked up 233 men, about one-third of the men who were in the water.[19] The decision to leave was exceptionally difficult for Lieutenant Commander Karpe to make, but it was based on a realistic appraisal of the situation, and was supported by Commanders Crouch, Abernethy, and McConnell. As the destroyer steamed through the knots of drifting sailors, they either called out plaintively to be saved or cursed the ship for leaving them. Soon their feeble cries were lost in the destroyer's wake and were heard no more.

CHAPTER 10

Epilogue

For three days the *Whipple* steamed toward Fremantle, Lieutenant Commander Karpe reducing speed to conserve the ship's shrinking fuel supply.[1] On 2 March Commanders Abernethy and McConnell counted heads and tallied the grim reaper's price for the *Langley*'s failed mission. Of the officers and men who had been aboard the *Pecos,* Abernethy had lost about 71 percent of his expanded crew and McConnell had lost at least 67 percent. About half the officers from both ships were rescued against about 33 percent of the enlisted men.[2]

Among the missing were Doctors Handley and Holly from the *Langley,* who were last seen tending wounded on the main deck. Lieutenant Stone was last seen by Engelman, who recalled that the lieutenant had part of one ear blown off. Stone was shaking a fist at the Japanese as Engelman went over the side. Ensign Crotty, who had been concussed by one of the forward bomb hits, never left the ship. His body was seen lying on the main deck by Ensign Emmanuel, who picked up Crotty's cap before leaving the ship. Nat Frey, the *Langley*'s engineering officer, was seen by Commander Divoll drifting alone on a shoring timber. Divoll invited Frey to join his group, but Frey preferred to remain alone. Later, Ensign Martin joined Frey on the spar and was with him when the *Whipple* showed up. Martin reached the destroyer but Frey was not seen again.

Also missing was Lieutenant Commander McPeak, whose last-minute machine-gunning of the strafer earned him a commendation. Most of the survivors recall that McPeak went down with the ship, but in fact he did get off. Ensign Martin saw him slide forward, away from the machine gun as the stern rose. Lieutenant Armbrust jumped with McPeak from the fantail, and Robert Foley saw the exec in the water thirty minutes after the *Pecos* went down. What happened to him after that is not known, but it may be safely assumed that he died like Baumker and Butts while saving others.

Wounds probably kept Gunner Anderson and Chief Pharmacist's Mate Wetherell from making it, as was the case for many others. Quartermaster Berry, Lieutenant McCall's assistant, disappeared as did Machinist Czado and "Jughaid" Crider. Leland Leonard and George Copeland from the *Langley*'s radio crew were left behind. Chief Gunner's Mate Timmons, who had helped Doyle drive out the round jammed in the number-six gun, was lost. Pay-clerk Randall, the man who spilled the money on the water, and Richard Ratajik, who had been with Kennedy when Randall dropped two bags of money to them, were also missing. The lists of the missing contain 456 names, and the lists are incomplete.[3]

On 4 March the *Whipple* reached Fremantle, her fuel nearly exhausted. After clearing the rescue area Lieutenant Commander Karpe had repeatedly reduced speed in order to stretch his dwindling fuel, and during the last twenty-four hours he had dispensed with zig-zagging, heading instead straight for the port along the shortest route. According to one account the destroyer actually ran out of fuel as she approached the dock. Though that did not happen, the fact is that the *Whipple* just squeaked by, and the last several hours were very tense as she crawled along toward Fremantle.

For the 233 survivors of the *Pecos* sinking, the arrival in Fremantle was the end of a nightmarish experience. As they trooped down the gangplank, partially clothed, oil-smeared, and exhausted, every one knew how lucky he was. As many as 500 of their shipmates had not been so lucky, and the figure was probably higher. The exact number of men who died may never be known, because the number of men aboard the *Pecos* when she left Tjilatjap was nearly twice her normal complement of 125. The extra men were survivors from several ships, and Commander Abernethy was not sure who all of them were. He pointed out in his report that because his executive officer and all his yeomen were missing, it was impossible to submit an accurate list of those who were missing.

Commander Abernethy's problem resulted from one sinking, whereas Commander McConnell had to sort out casualties from two sinkings. As a result, there are at least sixteen crewmen unaccounted for in his report, as well as eleven enlisted airmen.[4]

In his official report, Commander McConnell mentions and lists twenty-four crewmen killed, missing, or wounded when the Langley was abandoned. That figure matches the one provided in Doctor Blackwell's report, although the distribution between killed and injured is quite different, and the doctor did not include the missing. Included in the latter category would be the men who were blown or jumped overboard from the poop deck. Not included in any of those figures are the eleven Army enlisted men, who probably died as a result of hits two and three. Based on survivor interviews, it appears that there were actually fifty to sixty casualties on the 27th. Those figures agree with the numbers provided in the two reports and the Whipple's log. Adding the sixteen men who were known to have been on the ship, but whose names do not appear on any lists, raises the number to sixty.[5]

Inaccuracies and oversights in his official report caused Commander McConnell some embarrassment and very nearly got him into trouble. In his report, McConnell stated that "the Langley sank in a position seventy-four miles south of Tjilatjap, Java." Penciled in the lower margin below McConnell's statement is a question. "How do you know she sank?" The man who asked the question was Admiral Glassford.

The admiral's question was, of course, a reminder that no one had actually seen the tender go down, and he clearly felt that the ship had been abandoned too quickly. On 4 April he attached the first endorsement to McConnell's report, addressed to the Secretary of the Navy. In the endorsement he said:

> An examination of this report makes it doubtful that every effort was made to save the USS Langley and that her abandonment and subsequent endeavors to assure her sinking failed to uphold the best traditions of the naval service.

This bombshell went to Admiral Ernest King, then Commander in Chief, United States Fleet and the Chief of Naval Operations. Admiral King did not accept Glassford's view of the incident and directed him to explain more fully the basis for his opinion. At the same time, he directed McConnell to describe in greater detail the circumstances that caused him to abandon the *Langley*. McConnell responded with a seven-page, handwritten report that emphasized the threat of a renewed air attack and the danger that the ship might roll over.

> The *Langley*'s list was increasing and it appeared that unless the crew were cleared from the ship that a large loss of life would result should it capsize.

> The above considerations, particularly what appeared to be the imminent danger of capsizing led the commanding officer to order the crew over the side . . . the *Langley* was heeling progressively: rapidly at first to 10° then slowly to 15°–18° when abandoned . . . . Presuming the bombers to have been launched from an airfield in Bali more attacks could be anticipated that day as there was ample daylight remaining and the weather was ideal . . . . There were available two destroyers still intact and capable of taking off the large crew of the *Langley* but whose sole defense against high level bombing lay in their maneuverability. Their mission was to screen the *Langley* from submarine attack and they were useless against high flying aircraft and of but doubtful value against dive bombers or torpedo planes. Their presence represented an additional responsibility.

> It was assumed that an interval of two hours was available, free from air attack after the first attack, and that any rescue measures would have to be accomplished in the minimum of time.

McConnell also addressed the question raised by Admiral Glassford about whether or not anyone had seen the ship go down.

> Paragraph 17 of basic report is in error in that it gives the impression that the *Langley* was observed to sink. The report was prepared aboard the USS *Mount Vernon* while en route from Fremantle to Adelaide, Australia, and was based on conclusions drawn from radio messages. The Dutch Catalina which reported the *Langley* sunk gave the location as approximately that of the last observed position of the *Langley*.

The supplemental report was forwarded to Admiral Glassford who added another endorsement and sent it on to Admiral King. Glassford was still not entirely satisfied with McConnell's reasons for abandoning the ship as quickly as he did. In part Glassford said that:

> The above mentioned circumstances may well have justified his decision, but in light of subsequent events doubt arose as to justification. It was because of this doubt that the best traditions of the service had been upheld in not standing by the *Langley* and continuing his efforts to *save* the ship with at least some of his ship's company, but in his continued effort to *sink* his ship, that I judged the matter should be cleared, and so recommended. . . . If the *Langley* could have been kept afloat by the continued effort of any of her personnel who might have stood by her, it is possible that she could have been brought into a port by assistance sent out from Tjilatjap. This opinion is based on the fact that no further bombing attacks are known by me to have been made on the *Langley* and it might be expected that the late hour would preclude further attack that day and that the *Sea Witch* which followed about 12 hours behind the *Langley* entered Tjilatjap the . . . following morning without incident, and departed safely the early morning of 2 March. Operations in the general area off the south coast of Java were extremely hazardous but the fact remains that many ships were able to clear the area safely for Australia and elsewhere.

To Commander McConnell's great relief, Admiral King rejected Glassford's views. His two-paragraph decision stated:

> The Commander in Chief has carefully considered this report and its endorsements. In his opinion the Commanding Officer of the *Langley* was confronted with the necessity for an immediate decision, under extremely difficult circumstances. While there may be a difference of opinion as to his judgement, his decision was reasonable and within his authority and responsibility as Commanding Officer.
>
> The Commander in Chief does not agree with the then Commander U.S. Naval Forces, Southwest Pacific, that there is a question as to whether or not the best traditions of the service were upheld. He recommends that this matter be considered closed, without prejudice in any form whatsoever to the record of Commander McConnell.

Admiral King was right and Glassford was wrong. Looking at Glassford's argument, there are several apparent holes in it. Had a ship been sent out from Tjilatjap to take the *Langley* in tow, there would have been a lapse of up to ten hours before the ship arrived.[6] If in the meantime the Japanese had already dispatched a second raid, one launched at 1230, those planes could be expected to arrive over the stricken ship and her escorts at sometime between 1430 and 1500. Clearly the *Langley* would have been an easy target, and the loss of life would have been very large.

No further attacks were made on the ship because the Japanese had written her off as a total loss. But Commander McConnell did not know that, and he had to expect another attack. Even at "that late hour" Lieutenants Adachi and Tanabata had ample time to land, rearm, and attack again. Even had he been assured that there would be no more Japanese attacks, McConnell was still faced with the problem of a steadily increasing list and no means to reduce or stop the flooding.

Assuming that there were no more attacks, and the tow ship joined the *Langley* before nightfall, how was the ship to be towed with her rudder jammed hard over right? True, McConnell was still unaware of the problem at 1335, but had he elected to stay, the problem would soon have been discovered. The fact is that the *Langley* was battered, broken, and sinking, and McConnell knew it. He had no choice but to abandon ship when he did.

Why did Admiral Glassford, an experienced seaman, apparently overlook those circumstances? The answer may, in part, stem from his own experience in a similar situation. On 9 October 1918, while he was commanding the USS *Shaw* ((DD-68), the HMS *Aquitania* rammed his ship. The force of the collision tore away the *Shaw*'s bow. Flooding, afire, and threatened by explosion, the destroyer seemed doomed. But Glassford refused to abandon his ship, and "by his . . . resolute persistence. . . . the *Shaw* was saved . . . ."[7] The young skipper was awarded the Distinguished Service Medal. In view of his own experience, Glassford obviously felt that the effort to save the *Langley* had been lacking in "resolute persistence."

In marked contrast to the sharp questions raised by Admiral Glassford about Commander McConnell's actions, Commander Abernethy was awarded the Navy Cross for his actions during the bombing of the *Pecos*. His citation said:

> For extraordinary heroism as Commanding Officer of the USS
> *Pecos* during the bombardment and sinking of that vessel by enemy

Japanese airforces off Christmas Island on March 1, 1942. Putting up a desperate fight against successive waves of hostile dive bombers which swept down out of the sun, Commander Abernethy, although his ship was mercilessly overwhelmed by exploding bombs and strafing machine guns, kept her engines operating and her guns blasting away, until accumulated damage eventually opened her to the sea. Thereafter, calmly remaining aboard as the vessel settled forward, he directed abandon ship operations under a blistering hail of fire from ruthless enemy flyers who kept circling back to shell the helpless survivors huddled on life rafts and floating debris. His courageous and inspiring devotion to duty, maintained with utter disregard of personal safety, was in keeping with the highest traditions of the United States Naval Service.[8]

Commander Abernethy was not the only man cited for his actions. In his report, Abernethy cited fourteen *Pecos* and *Langley* crewmen for courageous acts. Of those fourteen, half survived, and the seven who were lost were all from the *Pecos*. The seven were: Lieutenant Commander McPeak; Lieutenant Stone, who had previously been commended by the commanding officer of the USS *Stewart* for courageous conduct; two warrant officers, Boatswain Baumker and Machinist Czado; three enlisted men, Chief Machinist's Mate A.L. Hagel, Machinist's Mate Second Class Schuler, who as the "best man" had repaired and restarted the critical main cargo pump, and Fireman First Class Marchand, who died next to Abernethy on the bridge.

Pecos survivors who were given recognition were Lieutenant Joseph L. LaComb, Chief Storekeeper Saxton for remaining on the bridge despite his wounds, and Storekeeper Third Class H.D. Metz for exposing himself to enemy fire while manning a machine gun. The four *Langley* survivors cited were Chief Yeoman G.J. Peluso for assisting the bridge force, Reginald Mills and Roy McNabb for manning guns under fire, and Robert Christensen for jumping into the fire-filled forward hold.

Similar to Admiral Glassford's criticism about the haste with which the *Langley* was abandoned was the wide-spread criticism voiced by the enlisted men concerning leaving Donovan behind. Many of the men felt that Commander Crouch should have sent one of the destroyers back for him. Those who supported that opinion argued that a destroyer could run in and get back out before the Japanese came back. Given their distance from Christmas Island at that time, and the speed at which a destroyer could operate unencumbered by the *Pecos,* their idea appeared to have merit.

Based on the *Whipple's* log, it would have required less than an hour for the destroyer to return to the island from the safety of the rain squall. In all probability, Donovan would have come out in the phosphate company's launch to meet the ship, so that the run in and the pick up would not have taken more than an hour. Admittedly, going back would have exposed the ship, its crew, and nearly 300 *Langley* survivors to the danger of another air attack during the run in and the run back out. But the advocates of a rescue attempt argue that the danger was the same whether they went back or steamed on.

The flying time for a Nell bomber from Bali to Christmas Island was about four hours.[9] If the Japanese had sent a second strike out in response to a sighting report at 1020, then those bombers would be nearly half way to their target at the time the *Whipple* was picking up Donovan. As the bombers closed on the target, the destroyer would be moving away at a rate of about 1/9th that of the bombers. Assuming that the bombers arrived two hours behind the *Whipple,* the destroyer would only be about forty nautical miles away and moving down a course that the Japanese may have already calculated. At some time between twenty and thirty minutes after crossing Christmas Island, the Japanese would have caught up with the *Whipple.*

On the other hand, moving south at 10 knots with the *Pecos* meant that at about the time the Japanese would reach Christmas Island, the fugitives would still only be about forty nautical miles south of the Island. Either way—go get Donovan or stay with the *Pecos*—the *Whipple* would be in about the same place at about the same time.

It would, therefore, seem that the risks were about the same either way, and that the humanitarian thing to have done would have been to make an attempt to recover Donovan. But there were other considerations that dictated against going back. For example, Donovan might not be able to come out to the ship. He might be dead. There was also the chance that a second Japanese attack might already be approaching the island, in which case the *Whipple* would walk right into it. Similar to the threat posed by the possibility of an air attack was the suspected presence of a submarine near the harbor entrance.[10]

There was another factor that entered into the calculations. The *Whipple* was very low on fuel and was scheduled to meet a tanker at the Cocos Islands after she transferred her passengers to the *Pecos*. A high-speed run to the island and out would have seriously depleted the ship's small fuel supply and would have jeopardized her chances of reaching the tanker. The decision was a tough one for Commander Crouch to make, but he really had no choice. One man was not worth the increased risks to the ship and the people in her.

Another, probably tougher, decision was made by Lieutenant Commander Karpe when he ordered his ship out of the rescue area at 2205 "due to submarine danger." Unlike the Donovan issue, few survivors doubted the need to get away, though leaving several hundred shipmates to die was a bitter pill. A few have since argued that the decision should have been delayed, but the facts support Lieutenant Commander Karpe.

The initial contact made at 2141 was reported as the sound of a submarine's propellers, a more positive identification than one based on sonar.[11] Additionally, several survivors said that they had been told by others that a submarine's conning tower was seen during the night, shortly prior to the *Whipple*'s arrival. But there were no first-hand accounts of a sighting given by the survivors who were interviewed. Similarly, Commander Divoll said that as he came aboard the *Whipple*, two flares exploded on the port side and a voice shouted, "Look at that S.O.B. there." Divoll did not see anything, but he was later told that a submarine had broached alongside the destroyer. There is, however, no report of such an incident in the *Whipple*'s log. Two survivors told reporters that they saw torpedo wakes that passed directly under the destroyer shortly before she got under way and dropped depth charges. Again there is no report of that in the *Whipple*'s log. At 2156 contact was made again; this time propellers were heard, and the sub was picked up on sonar.[12]

There is no doubt that the *Whipple* had located a submarine, and the reports of men having seen a conning tower may be true. Whether or not one broached alongside, or fired torpedoes, is less certain. Such events would have been so dramatic that more than just a few should have recalled them. Still, they cannot be discounted entirely, since there exists the possibility that in the excitement of getting under way, most of the men failed to see them.

In view of the deteriorating situation and the obvious intention on the part of the British and most of the Americans to get out of the Netherlands East Indies, was the attempt to send the *Langley* and the *Sea Witch* to Java worthwhile or should they have been sent to India with Convoy MS-5? Had the *Langley* delivered her ready-to-fly P-40s on the 28th, according to the original schedule, the planes might have gotten into the air. Though the Japanese invasion would not have been stopped, it might have been more costly to them. It is an unfortunate fact of war that men and equipment are expendable, and as long as a reasonable possibility existed that the *Langley* could deliver her planes, there was little reason to call off the attempt. It was, after all, not the mission per se that caused the *Langley*'s loss, but the back-and-forth changes that occurred on the 26th that effectively eliminated her nighttime cover.

On the other hand, had the tender been diverted to India— either with Convoy MS-5, or at any time until 26 February—it would have made no difference in the outcome of the battle for Java. In fact, the planes would have been much more useful to the 51st and 35th groups in India than to the island's defenders. But there was a political consideration to be made, and the United States may have been reluctant to antagonize even a weak ally so early in the war.

The situation was in many ways similar to what went on between Great Britain and France during the battle of France in 1940. The French wanted British fighters moved forward into France, but the British refused to do that, save for a few Hurricane squadrons. As a result, the French harbored the belief that the British had not made their fullest effort and had essentially abandoned them. There is no doubt that the Dutch, who were convinced that the island could be held, had much the same opinion about their allies in Java. In those circumstances, withholding the planes might have created a rift between America and the Dutch that could have affected future operations.

Thus from a tactical, or political, point of view, there was little else to do but send in the *Langley* and her planes. On the other hand, the *Sea Witch* should have been sent on to India despite the Dutch protest on 18 and 19 February. By the 22nd, the situation in Java was falling apart so rapidly that there was no hope of assembling those twenty-seven planes in time to use them.

Admiral Glassford, in his criticism of Commander McConnell, pointed out that the *Sea Witch* had reached Tjilatjap safely on the 28th. What he did not say was that the freighter had been allowed to keep to the original schedule and had approached the harbor under the cover of darkness. But the fact that she arrived did not do any good since her cargo of P-40s did not even reach the dock. By 1 March the twenty-seven crated fighters had been unloaded and set aboard lighters. That day the Japanese landed on both ends of the island, and all thought of assembling the planes was set aside. On 2 March the *Sea Witch* escaped to sea while the twenty-seven P-40s were destroyed in their crates.[13] The fact that the ship escaped to safety was simply a matter of good luck, and the loss of her cargo was a complete waste.

The attempt to supply fighters to Java by sea in order to avoid the losses suffered by flying them there had ended in failure. The losses had been 100 percent of the aircraft and nearly 96 percent of the pilots and ground crews.

In his handwritten report, Commander McConnell suggested that the Japanese knew about the *Langley*'s mission and essentially ambushed her. Many of the survivors who were interviewed are still convinced that a spy in Fremantle tipped off the Japanese. It is a possibility that cannot be proved or disproved. The *Langley* had transmitted on the evening of 26 February asking for air cover. It is probable that she was located by radio direction finders and the patrol plane was sent out to find her. Masatake Okumiya says that an intelligence estimate of the *Langley*'s mission was made *after* she was sunk.[14] If that is the case, then her sinking was a to-be-expected result of the attempt to approach the coast in broad daylight, and not an ambush.

On the night of 4 March, none of the enlisted survivors were

Apparently in the belief that anyone who had been sunk twice in two days in the Pacific would be better off in the Atlantic, the Navy sent most of the *Langley* survivors to a subchaser school in Florida. *PC-500* was one of their training boats. (National Archives)

asking questions about any of the decisions that had been made. They were all glad to be alive and ashore. That evening the last act in the money-on-the-water episode was played out in Fremantle. Lester Bates, who had grabbed a bundle of Australian pound notes before boarding the *Whipple* the first time, came aboard the second time empty-handed. He found his friend in the *Whipple*'s fire room and told him he was broke, whereupon the fireman split his half with Bates. When they landed in Fremantle, the sailors were issued Australian Army uniforms and housed overnight at an Australian Army camp. Bates and several others slipped out of camp and spent all of Bates's money in town. At the end of the wild night, Bates observed that his earlier generosity had been the "best investment" he had ever made.

The following morning, nearly all the survivors went aboard the USS *Mt. Vernon* for transportation to the United States. Eleven were reported as "absent from muster and they are not on board for assignment—their whereabouts is unknown."[15] Ten others stayed in Australia for immediate assignment. Of the eleven unaccounted for, ten of them subsequently turned up on ships in the Southwest Pacific, and one was never seen again. It appears that the ten were simply lost in the bureaucratic shuffle and had been legitimately reassigned. What happened to the eleventh man is anybody's guess.

After the *Mt. Vernon* reached San Francisco on 31 March, most of the men were sent on thirty-day leave and reassigned to a subchaser school in Miami, Florida. A handful died during the war, including Army Lieutenant Akerman who was killed in a training accident in 1943.[16] Several enlisted men were commissioned, among them Charles Snay, John Kennedy, and Claud Hinds.

Some of the officers held commands during the war and after. Abernethy commanded the USS *President Jackson*, an attack transport, and after the war, the USS *Tucson*. Abernethy retired a rear admiral in 1951. McConnell commanded a carrier during the war, and retired a vice admiral. He died in 1977. Divoll commanded an attack transport, the USS *Fillmore*, and retired a captain in 1947. Ensign Ditto commanded the destroyer escort USS *O'Toole* at the end of the war. Ensign Emmanuel changed over to naval aviation and flew PBY "Black Cats" in the Netherlands East Indies and the Philippines.

A few survivors were discharged for medical reasons as a result of wounds suffered during the two sinkings. Earl Snyder never fully recovered and was retired in 1945. Carl Onberg hung on, but his injuries caught up with him in 1958 and he too was retired on a disability.

A handful of the survivors had notable experiences during the war. After being released from a hospital in Australia, Gerald Dix flew combat missions in New Guinea with a P-39 outfit and was later sent to Europe. Two days after D-day, while strafing a train near Bordeaux, France, his P-47 hit a power line and crashed. Dix was captured by the Germans and spent the rest of the war as a POW.

James Mealley made boatswain's mate first class in 1944 and took command of a brand new garbage lighter, YG-34, in Port Arthur, Texas. After delivering ammunition to New Orleans, Mealley and his ten-man crew sailed the lighter to San Diego. During the trip they battled heavy winds, forty-foot seas, and navigated with a faulty compass. The crew quickly dubbed the YG-34 "the garbage scow with a plow bow." The feat received national coverage in the press, and was written up in a post-war Navy training manual.[17]

The Koepsell brothers, Chester and Norman, were the only two Langley crewmen to be assigned to the new Langley, an aircraft carrier, CVL-27. As a part of Task Force 38, the new Langley concentrated on the destruction of enemy air power and air installations in the Formosa-Pescadores-Ryukyus area and along the Indochina coast to Saigon. The ship was damaged during an air attack near Okinawa on 20 January 1945. The Koepsells escaped injury in their third encounter with Japanese bombers.

At least one other survivor was, like Dix, a victim of the Germans. During the invasion of Sicily, Walter Sinner was on a sub-chaser that was bombed and sunk by a German JU-88. Sinner was seriously injured by shrapnel, but recovered and retired from the Navy in 1965. James Saulton and Henry Restorff served in minesweepers during the D-day landings at Omaha Beach, but unlike Sinner they came through unscathed.

The Whipple spent the rest of the war escorting convoys in the Pacific until mid-1943 when she was sent to similar duty in the

Atlantic. For a brief period in 1944 the old destroyer was part of a hunter-killer task group formed around the USS *Guadalcanal* (CVE-60). It was during that time, and later in 1944 while escorting Convoy UGS-36, that the *Whipple* fought the Germans. In 1945 she was reclassified an auxiliary ship (AG-117), and spent her last few months as a submarine target ship. Her stripped hulk was sold for scrap in 1947.

The *Phoenix* survived the war and was sold to Argentina in 1951. Her name was changed to the *General Belgrano*. On 2 May 1982, forty years after she had escorted the *Langley* out of Fremantle, she became the first warship to fall victim to a nuclear submarine. During the undeclared war over the Falkland Islands, HMS *Conqueror* hit the ex-*Phoenix* with two tigerfish torpedoes and sank her.

It would be an exaggeration to say that the *Langley*'s loss had a profound influence on the subsequent conduct of the war. But certainly her loss, and the surrounding circumstances, had a contributory effect. From the start, Admiral King had been against placing U.S. ships under foreign command. He also did not like mixed commands in which ships of two or more foreign navies operated as a combined, tactical unit. The ABDA experience, and Dutch mismanagement, confirmed for him the soundness of his views.[18]

The *Langley*'s loss was representative of what could happen when U.S. ships operated under foreign command. It is not surprising, therefore, that Admiral King used his position on the Joint Chiefs of Staff to ensure that U.S. ships would not only be free of foreign control, but would not again come under the authority of a single supreme commander. In effect, the Pacific war became an American responsibility, and in 1944 Admiral King successfully opposed using the British fleet as a part of the American operations.[19]

The *Langley* was gone, and directly or indirectly she had taken the *Pecos* and the *Edsall* with her. Three ships and over 700 men were lost, victims of events that were beyond their control. Despite the enormous odds against them, and in the face of a hopeless situation, every man in those three ships did his best, each man did his duty. Eighty years earlier General Thomas "Stonewall" Jackson, CSA, in a similarly hopeless situation said, "Duty is ours; consequences are God's." And so it was for the crews of the *Langley*, the *Pecos* and the *Edsall*.

Tables of Specifications— USS *Langley* and USS *Pecos*

USS *Langley* AV-3

Coal Collier 1913–1920 USS *Jupiter* AC-3
Aircraft Carrier 1922–1936 USS *Langley* CV-1
Seaplane Tender 1937–1942 USS *Langley* AV-3

Dimensions for AV-3	
Overall Length	542'
Beam	65'
Mean Draught	21'3"
Max. Displacement	14,500 T
Max. Speed in 1942	13K

Flight Deck	
Length	319'9"
Width	65'
Height	56'

Armament
(4) 5" x 51 cal.
(4) 3" x 50 cal.
(4) .50 cal. mg.

Power Plant: G.E. Turbo/Elect. (D.C.), 2 Shafts, 7000 h.p. 3 Boilers + 1 Aux., Generator Sets 5

Accommodations (Normal)
Officers 54   Warrant Officers 10   Enlisted Men 648

Source: Ships Data, U.S. Naval Vessels, 1 January 1942
          Naval Historical Center, Washington, D.C.

USS *Pecos* AO-6

Fleet Oiler 1921–1942

Dimensions

Overall Length	475'7"
Beam	56'3"
Mean Draught	26'8"
Displacement	14,800 T
Max. Speed in 1942	14K

Armament

(4) 5" x 51 cal.

(2) 3" x 50 cal. AA

(10) .50 cal. mg.

Power Plant: Reciprocating Steam, 2 Shafts, 6000 h.p. 4 B&W Boilers

Accommodations (Normal)

All Ranks 125

Source: Jane's Fighting Ships, 1924

Source Notes

An abbreviated form has been used in the source notes to save space. Complete publishing information, or location, is given in the bibliography.

Chapter 1

[1]Office of Naval Intelligence, "Attack on U.S. Naval Vessels by Japanese Airplanes," undated, p. 1. (Hereafter cited as ONI Report); "Kokan Senshi Nr. 26." Unless otherwise noted, all material about the Japanese attack on the *Langley* comes from these sources.

[2]Masatake Okumiya et al., *Zero*, pp. 55–56.

[3]Paul St. Pierre, correspondence and private papers.

[4]Ibid.

[5]Navy Department, *Dictionary of American Naval Fighting Ships*, vol. IV, p. 45; and Oscar Parkes and Francis E. McMurtrie, eds., *Jane's Fighting Ships*, 1924, p. 389.

[6]Joe C. Cline, "First Naval Aviation Unit in France," *Naval Aviation in World War I*, p. 12.

[7]Charles M. Melhorn, *Two Block Fox: The Rise of the Aircraft Carrier, 1922–1929*, p. 36.

[8]Chief of Naval Operations, *United States Naval Aviation 1910–1970*, pp. 287–88.

[9]Jackson R. Tate, "We Rode the Covered Wagon," U.S. Naval Institute *Proceedings*, October 1978.

[10]Ibid, p. 69.

[11]Ibid.

[12]*New York Times*, 16 April 1923.

[13]Charlie Bolka correspondence.

[14]George Van Duers correspondence.

[15]Charlie Bolka correspondence.

[16]The Rodgers Family Papers.

[17]CNO, *United States Naval Aviation 1910–1970*, p. 57.

[18]Tate, "We Rode the Covered Wagon."

[19]Earl Gainer correspondence.

[20]"USS *Langley*, Seaplane Tender" visitor's brochure, May 1939.

[21]Howard Whan interview.

[22]Abernethy, E. Paul, "The Pecos Died Hard," U.S. Naval Institute *Proceedings*, December 1969, p. 76.

[23]Michel Emmanuel interview and private papers.

Chapter 2

[1]The Dutch officer was Lieutenant General H. ter Poorten. Major General L. H. Brereton, USA, was ABDAAIR until 28 January 1942 when he was relieved by Air Marshall Sir Richard E. C. Peirse. F. C. Van Oosten, *The Battle of the Java Sea*, p. 15.

[2]William Glassford, "Narrative of Events in the South West Pacific, 14 February–5 April 1942." (Hereafter cited as Glassford Report.)

[3]Walter D. Edmonds, *They Fought With What They Had*, p. 250.

[4]Van Oosten, pp. 95–98.

[5]Edmonds, pp. 278–79.

[6]Ibid., p. 326.

[7]Operations, Java Campaign, Document 714.

[8]When Admiral Glassford referred to that situation in his report he may not have been on firm ground, and in fact may not have known most, or all, of the real details. There is some evidence that as early as 9 February, the Army Air Force was planning to send the *Langley* and the thirty-two ready-to-fly P-40s to India. Under the circumstances it is easily understood why the admiral was unsure of the tender's destination until the last minute. Glassford Report and Edmonds, p. 348.

[9]Homer L. Sanders, diary entry for 22 February 1942.

[10]Gerald Dix interview.

[11]Clearly Major Sanders thought the *Langley*'s P-40s were his, which if true made the tender a part of the convoy. On 14 February a radio message reported the *Phoenix* to be escorting a portion of Convoy MS-5 to Fremantle. The implication was that the rest of MS-5—the *Langley*—would be picked up in Fremantle. A 23 February Army message indicated that when the *Langley* was detached from MS-5 on 22 February, she had been considered a part of Convoy MS-5 en route to India. Convoy and Routing Files, 10th Fleet, Convoy MS-5; and Operations, Java Campaign, Document 740.

[12]Gerald Dix interview.

[13]Operations, Java Campaign, Documents 708 and 740.

[14]Ibid., Document 757.

[15]Glassford Report.

[16]Edmonds, p. 416.

[17]According to Admiral Glassford, General Wavell's views "were well known," and on 20 February he recommended to London that "the defense of Java cease as of a certain day. . ."

[18]Edmonds, p. 270.

[19]Edmonds, p. 416 and Operations, Java Campaign, Document 737.

[20]Operations, Java Campaign, Document 735.

[21]Ibid., Documents 937 and 946.

[22]Gordon Spence interview and Gerald Dix interview.

[23]Gordon Spence interview and Ross Hoyt interview. There is no known record of who the twelve replacements were. When casualty lists

and survivor lists from the *Langley* and *Pecos* sinkings were sent to COM-SOWESPAC, the pilots were listed but the enlisted men were not. McConnell did not include any of the Army Air Force men in either his casualty list or his survivor list.

[24]Edmonds, pp. 366–67.

[25]Glassford Report.

Chapter 3

[1]Samuel Eliot Morison, *The Rising Sun in the Pacific*, pp. 359–60.

[2]Homer Sanders, diary entry for 23 February 1942; and "Combat Narratives: The Java Sea Campaign" Copy No. 527, p. 45. (Hereafter cited as "Combat Narratives No. 527".)

[3]Robert P. McConnell. "Operations, Actions, and Sinking of USS *Langley*, 22 February–5 March 1942" (hereafter cited as the McConnell Report); and Homer Sanders, diary entry for 25 February 1942.

[4]Glassford apparently found out about the change on the 25th—three days after the event. Glassford Report; and "Combat Narratives No. 527," p. 45.

[5]Glassford Report.

[6]Van Oosten, p. 15.

[7]Ibid., p. 15.

[8]The admiral was not alone in that belief, and many accounts about the *Langley*'s last trip state that her destination after leaving Fremantle was Ceylon. The situation was, and is, indicative of the confusion that characterized the whole plan.

[9]Glassford Report.

[10]Operations, Java Campaign, Document 740.

[11]Ibid., Document 741.

[12]Glassford Report.

[13]Ibid.

[14]Ibid.

[15]McConnell said it was a minelayer, but Samuel E. Morison and several others described the ship as a minesweeper. The important thing is that he was diverted from the original plan—again.

[16]Glassford Report.

[17]Ibid.

[18]Lawrence Divoll interview.

[19]It is not intended that the crewmen be depicted as having a "careless" attitude. In fact, they all were concerned about the sighting, but very few realized what it portended. Nearly all the survivors interviewed said that they gave little thought to the sighting or the probable consequences.

[20]Tom Spence's optimism was typical of the attitude of the crew.

[21]All the material about McLean, Riley, and Wetherbee comes from a twenty-eight page narrative written by Wetherbee in 1964, when he was

contacted by a former shipmate who wanted information about the ship. Frank Wetherbee papers.

[22]Gerald Dix interview.

[23]There are two versions, a long and a short, of this announcement. There is also some difference of opinion over whether it was made on the evening of the 26th or on the morning of the 27th. The version given here was obtained from Lawrence Divoll, and the time was established on the basis of majority opinion.

Chapter 4

[1]Reginald Mills interview.

[2]Lawrence Divoll interview. Another source, Lester Bates, described the fire control system as being much more primitive. According to Bates it consisted of a pair of binoculars and a plumb bob. None of the other survivors could recall what it was, but a few had a dim recollection of the one described in the text.

[3]The conversation and Ditto's actions are from Michel Emmanuel, "The Java Crapshoot," *Shipmate*, June 1972, pp. 19–20.

[4]The G3M Nell had no internal bomb racks. The center section exterior racks could carry twelve 60-kg (132-lb.) bombs, or two 250-kg (551-lb.) bombs, or one 500-kg (1,202-lb.) bomb. There was also provision for a single 800-kg (1,764-lb.) torpedo. On this raid, the planes carried just one 250-kg bomb each. ONI Report; and Rene J. Francillon, *Japanese Navy Bombers of World War II*, p. 62.

[5]All references to radio transmissions in this chapter are from McConnell Report, Enclosure C, "*Langley* Radio Log."

[6]McConnell Report.

[7]Ibid.

[8]Jones was unaware what a close call he had until he read Commander McConnell's report in 1980.

[9]Details about the engine room and the fire rooms were obtained from Lawrence Divoll, Chester Koepsell, Richard Shanley, and Raymond Shepston.

[10]The term was used by Lieutenant Frey and is recorded in the McConnell Report.

[11]Chester Koepsell said that the water did not rush in like something out of a disaster movie, but rose slowly as though it was "seeping through the hull." Chester Koepsell interview.

[12]All references to Japanese actions in this chapter are taken from: ONI Report; and "Kokan Senshi Nr. 26."

[13]McConnell Report.

[14]Emmanuel, "The Java Crapshoot," p. 19; and Walter Karig and Welbourne Kelly, *Battle Report: Pearl Harbor to the Coral Sea*, p. 223.

[15]Earl Snyder interview.

[16]McConnell Report, Radio Log.

[17]This assumption is based on survivor interviews, during which several survivors reported having seen dead or injured Army Air Force men in that area. Since, with the exception of Akerman and Dix, all the Army pilots escaped the *Langley* without injury, it follows that the Army men who were seen on the main deck were enlisted men. Other than the few pilots who were acting as lookouts, it appears that the Army personnel went to their planes when general quarters was sounded. There are even stories about one pilot trying to take off, but they appear to be legend based on misconceptions.

[18]Henry Restorff interview and Marvin Snyder interview.

[19]Charles Snay later saw Gunner Anderson being carried to the rail when the ship was abandoned. He said that Anderson was completely incoherent and helpless. Since Anderson and Soke are the only two reported casualties on gun number-two, it is assumed that Anderson was the one whose cloths were blown off, as described in: George van Deurs, "Last Cruise of the *Langley*," *V.F.W. Magazine*, April 1962, p. 15.

[20]Henry Restorff interview.

[21]Millard McKinney interview and Chester Koepsell interview.

[22]Millard McKinney interview.

[23]Robert Blackwell, "USS *Langley*," undated, typewritten report.

[24]Michel Emmanuel, interview, correspondence, and "The Java Crapshoot," p. 19.

[25]Millard McKinney interview. McKinney admits that he may be wrong about the minimum pressure needed, but "whatever it was, we didn't have it."

[26]Based on identified casualties and Blackwell, "USS *Langley*."

[27]Millard McKinney interview.

[28]Blackwell, "USS *Langley*."

[29]Charles Snay interview. There is no record in the *Langley*'s radio log of this message having been sent, but Snay says that he clearly recalls writing it out and giving it to the four operators.

[30]McConnell Report.

[31]John Kennedy Interview

[32]The Japanese claimed to have shot down two flying boats near the *Langley*. Apparently a gunner in one of the Allied planes nailed a Zero. ONI Report.

[33]This differs from McConnell's report substantially, and is based on the unanimous agreement among the survivors that the ship started to lose way almost immediately after being bombed. Divoll and Koepsell both said that Frey had shut down the motors shortly after the fifth hit.

Chapter 5

[1]All radio transmissions used in this chapter are taken from: McConnell Report and *Langley*'s Radio Log.

[2] This account of the engine room scene was obtained from Lawrence Divoll and is supported by Chester Koepsell.

[3] James Mealley interview. Several survivors found compartments flooded when they later tried to reach their quarters, and all recalled the river that flowed down the port well deck.

[4] McConnell Report.

[5] Michel Emmanuel, interview and correspondence.

[6] Divoll recalls, however, that the battle phone was working. Emmanuel says it was not, and Snay recalls that the entire interior communications system was gone. There is no doubt, however, that Divoll headed for the bridge at this time.

[7] Richard Shanley interview and Michel Emmanuel correspondence.

[8] Seller's actions are described in a lengthy narrative written by Emmanuel at the author's request.

[9] Jay Martin interview and Blackwell, "USS *Langley*."

[10] Blackwell, "USS *Langley*.

[11] McConnell Report, *Langley*'s Radio Log.

[12] Lawrence Divoll interview.

[13] McConnell estimated the airplanes' weight at 105 tons, which is about right for all thirty-two planes. But there were only twenty-seven planes on the flight deck, and they totaled just under ninety tons. McConnell Report.

[14] He was right about the narrow channel at Tjilatjap. In fact, Admiral Glassford was so concerned about it that he would not allow any ship to use it during an air raid, because he was afraid one would be sunk in the channel and block it. McConnell Report and Glassford Report.

[15] McConnell apparently never did know that his rudder was jammed. There is no mention of it in his handwritten, supplementary report. McConnell Report.

[16] Divoll interview.

[17] Raymond Shepston interview.

[18] McConnell Report, *Langley*'s Radio Log.

[19] Michel Emmanuel was unaware of this until he read McConnell's report in 1980. Michel Emmanuel correspondence and McConnell Report.

[20] Frank Wetherbee papers, Jim Mealley interview , and Lawrence Divoll interview.

[21] Lawrence Divoll interview.

[22] Ray Wagner, *American Combat Airplanes*, pp. 210–11.

[23] Lester Bates interview.

[24] He used several messengers for the job including Charles Snay. John Kennedy interview.

[25] Blackwell, "USS *Langley*."

[26] Details about the last several minutes in the engine room came from the Chester Koepsell interview.

[27] McConnell Report.

Chapter 6

[1]McConnell had ordered the ship abandoned at 1332, and the last man was fished out at 1358. The rescue had actually been under way since before 1325 as the result of the earlier abandonment. USS *Whipple*, Deck Log. (Hereafter cited as *Whipple* log.)

[2]In his handwritten, supplementary report, McConnell wrote that the list had reached 18 degrees. The torpedo rumor was widely believed, and some survivors still insist that the *Langley* was attacked by torpedo planes.

[3]Millard McKinney interview. Of all the survivors interviewed, McKinney had the most detailed recollection of the ship's interior.

[4]The figure is based on a drawing found in the 1940 edition of *The Blue Jacket's Manual*, and the recollections of James Mealley and John Bartuck.

[5]Marvin Snyder interview.

[6]The entire episode involving Ditto and Whan was obtained during the Howard Whan interview.

[7]All material about the man in the brig was obtained from Michel Emmanuel. The prisoner survived the war and was located, but he refused to take part in an interview.

[8]McConnell Report, *Langley*'s Radio Log.

[9]The account and conversation that follows were provided during the Earl Snyder interview.

[10]George Vano's actions, and the conversation that follows, are from the Frank Wetherbee papers.

[11]The money-on-the-water account, and the conversations, are a compilation of material from: the John Martin interview; the John Kennedy interview; and the Reginald Mills interview.

[12]James Harvey interview.

[13]Michel Emmanuel correspondence.

[14]The account that follows about recovering Lieutenant Bailey's body was compiled from the Gerald Dix interview and the Raymond Shepston interview.

[15]Lieutenant Bailey was buried at sea, the service being conducted by Commander Divoll.

[16]Divoll had already left the ship and was cruising among the swimmers in one of the *Whipple*'s whaleboats, picking up the weak and injured men. McConnell Report.

[17]*Whipple* Log and McConnell Report.

[18]*Whipple* Log.

Chapter 7

[1]James Moorehead interview.

[2]Abernethy "The *Pecos* Died Hard." There is a marked difference

between a fleet oiler, equipped to fuel ships at sea, and a tanker that is just a bulk carrier.

[3]Glassford Report. The account that follows of Admiral Glassford's attempts to get oil out of Java came from the same source.

[4]Abernethy, "The *Pecos* Died Hard." p. 77.

[5]Robert Foley interview and D. Harper interview.

[6]E. Paul Abernethy, "Action and Sinking of USS *Pecos*, 1 March 1942." (Hereafter cited as Abernethy Report.)

[7]McConnell Report and Michel Emmanuel correspondence.

[8]The conversation came from the James Moorehead interview.

[9]Ibid.

[10]Abernethy Report.

[11]Thomas Laforest interview and *Whipple* Log.

[12]McConnell Report.

[13]Abernethy Report and Carl Armbrust narrative.

[14]E. M. Crouch, "Narrative," 4 April 1944. (Hereafter cited as Crouch Narrative.)

[15]There had been thirty-three Army officers and twelve Army enlisted men aboard the *Langley*. Two pilots went to the *Edsall*. Thirty-one pilots and one mechanic went to the *Whipple*. Therefore, eleven airmen were unaccounted for. According to Dix all the pilots were reunited aboard the *Edsall* at Christmas Island, which means that the thirty-fourth man was a mechanic, as were the eleven missing airmen.

[16]*San Francisco Chronicle*, 4 April 1942.

[17]Abernethy Report, *Whipple* Log, and Navy Department, *Dictionary of American Naval Fighting Ships*, vol. II, p. 328.

[18]*Whipple* Log.

[19]Abernethy Report.

[20]Blackwell, "USS *Langley*;" and USS *Pecos*, survivors' narratives, "J. L. Yon narrative."

[21]USS *Pecos*, survivors' narratives, "R. L. Mayo narrative."

[22]Ibid., "Carl Armbrust narrative."

[23]Raymond Shepston interview.

[24]*San Francisco Chronicle*, 4 April 1942.

[25]Ibid.

[26]The account of Japanese actions that follows is taken from "Kokan Senshi Nr. 26."

[27]USS *Pecos*, survivors' narratives, "Francis McCall narrative."

[28]Ibid.

[29]USS *Pecos*, survivors' narratives, "J. Balitski narrative."

Chapter 8

[1]Unless otherwise noted, all activities attributed to *Pecos* crewmen were taken from the individual narratives contained in: USS *Pecos*, survivors' narratives, Naval Personnel Command.

[2]Unless otherwise noted all activities attributed to Japanese airmen were taken from: "Kokan Senshi Nr. 26."

[3]John Bartuck interview.

[4]Frank Doyle interview.

[5]Frank Wetherbee papers.

[6]Emmanuel, "The Java Crapshoot," p. 21.

[7]David Jones interview and Robert Foley interview.

[8]Emmanuel, "The Java Crapshoot," p. 21.

[9]*Whipple* Log.

[10]*New York Times*, 5 April 1942.

[11]Abernethy, "The *Pecos* Died Hard," p. 79; and Carl Armbrust interview.

[12]Abernethy, "The *Pecos* Died Hard," p. 80.

[13]Walter Sinner interview.

[14]John Martin interview.

[15]Christensen may have been a bigger hero than most people realized. Several *Langley* survivors recall seeing aerial torpedoes stowed below, and Commander Divoll said that when the fire broke out Abernethy told him that the hold contained "roughly 400 tons of aviation bombs with dunnage on top." Carl Armbrust recalled during the interview that the *Pecos* was carrying "a lot of ammunition." According to Armbrust the ammunition included torpedoes, torpedo warheads, 8-inch, and 6-inch rounds.

[16]The author was a tank gunner and later a tank commander. We were often told that the 90-mm HE round was "safe" until fired through the tube. The warhead was armed after the arming ring had rotated a predetermined number of revolutions as the round spiraled up the tube. The claim was strongly doubted after an accidentally dropped round exploded in another tank. The following conversation was obtained during the Frank Doyle interview.

[17]D. Harper interview.

[18]Frank Doyle interview.

[19]*Whipple* Log.

[20]J. L. Yon, "Doctors at Sea," *Colliers*, 28 August 1943, p. 21.

[21]Charles Snay interview.

[22]Abernethy, "The *Pecos* Died Hard," p. 80.

[23]Carl Armbrust interview.

Chapter 9

[1]All references to radio transmissions and the acts of individual *Pecos* crewmen are from: USS *Pecos*, survivors' narratives; and Abernethy Report.

[2]*Whipple* Log.

[3]Richard Shanley interview.

[4]Earl Snyder interview.

[5] Lawrence Divoll interview.

[6] John Martin interview. Ensign John "Jay" Martin deserves a lot more credit for his actions of 27 February–1 March 1942 than he received. Among the officers, Martin was one who performed his duty to the letter, and then some. He is an example of the thousands whose acts go unrecognized in wartime.

[7] E. Paul Abernethy interview.

[8] Abernethy does not recall being with anyone. This account is based on: Lawrence Divoll interview; and Charles Snay interview.

[9] *San Francisco Chronicle*, 4 April 1942.

[10] "The Death of the USS *Edsall*," *Shipmate*, April 1980, p. 12. Another source reports that five bodies were found in a POW camp in the Celebes that were identified as *Edsall* crewmen. Skip W. Harrington, "The Mystery of the USS *Edsall*," *Shipmate*, Jan.–Feb. 1980, p. 28.

[11] *Whipple* Log; Michel Emmanuel correspondence; and Robert Shanley interview.

[12] *Whipple* Log.

[13] Crouch narrative.

[14] John Kennedy interview.

[15] James Mealley interview.

[16] Harry Mayfield interview.

[17] Lester Bates, private papers.

[18] Millard McKinney interview.

[19] Most authorities give 220 as the number rescued. The 233 figure is based on the survivor lists, with Akerman and Dix added. The number does not include Donovan who was not aboard the *Pecos* when she went down.

Chapter 10

[1] *Whipple* Log.

[2] Based on a comparison of casualty and survivor lists from both ships.

[3] The eleven enlisted Army men are not listed, and at least sixteen *Langley* crewmen are unaccounted for. Abernethy pointed out in his report that his lists were not complete.

[4] Casualty lists and USS *Langley*, Muster Rolls.

[5] Eight dead (McConnell) plus 20 wounded (Blackwell) plus 5 missing (McConnell) plus 11 airmen plus 16 not accounted for (Muster rolls) equals 60. The figure for the missing airmen is arrived at in this way: 33 pilots plus 12 mechanics equals 45; minus 2 wounded pilots equals 43, minus 32 transferred to the *Edsall* at Christmas Island equals 11 unaccounted for.

[6] Assuming the *Langley* was seventy-five nautical miles offshore, and the tow ship could make 10 knots over the bottom, the travel time to the *Langley* would have been seven and a half hours. Add two and a half for

preparations, delays, and negotiating the channel, and ten hours seems a reasonable estimate.

[7]"Vice Admiral William A. Glassford, USN (deceased)."

[8]Abernethy's stubborn resistance must have struck a sympathetic chord in Glassford's heart. The admiral had commanded the oiler from May 1922 to January 1923. "Vice Admiral Glassford"; and E. Paul Abernethy papers.

[9]Based on the planes' performance figures and the demonstrated time from Bali to reach the *Langley*. Francillon, *Japanese Navy Bombers of World War II*, p. 62.

[10]McConnell Report.

[11]Thomas Laforest interview.

[12]*Whipple* Log.

[13]There are two versions of how the planes were destroyed. One says they were burned, and the other claims they were pushed off the lighters into the bay. The latter is probably true. Wesley F. Craven and James L. Cate, *The Army Air Force in World War II*, vol. 1, p. 398.

[14]Okumiya et al., *Zero*, p. 90.

[15]McConnell Report.

[16]Akerman was killed on 28 April 1943. He was strafing a target tank near Coyote Wells, California, when his P-38 "mushed into the ground." "Report of Aircraft Accident, Akerman William P. 1st. Lt. 2-28-43."

[17]James Mealley interview and private papers.

[18]Dr. Gerald Wheeler interview.

[19]Thomas Buell, *Master of Sea Power*, pp. 470–71, and Earnest King and Walter Whitehill, *Fleet Admiral King*, pp. 370–71.

Bibliography

Correspondence, Interviews, and Private Papers

Abernethy, E. Paul. USS *Pecos*. Interview, correspondence, and private papers.

Armbrust, Carl R. USS *Pecos*. Interview and correspondence.

Bartuck, John. USS *Langley*. Interview.

Bates, Lester. USS *Langley*. Interview, correspondence, and private papers.

Berkow, Joseph J. USAAF, Class 40-G. Interview.

Bolka, Charles. USS *Langley*. Correspondence and private papers.

Divoll, Lawrence. USS *Langley*. Interview and photos.

Dix, Gerald. 33rd Pursuit Squadron. Interview, correspondence, and photos.

Doyle, Frank. USS *Pecos*. Interview.

Eckstein, Eugene. USS *Langley*. Correspondence and photos.

Emmanuel, Michel. USS *Langley*. Interview, correspondence, and private papers.

Foley, Robert W. USS *Pecos*. Interview.

Gainer, Earl. USS *Langley*. Correspondence.

Harper, D. USS *Pecos*. Interview and photos.

Harvey, James. USS *Langley*. Interview.

Hoyt, Ross G. USAAF, Australia. Correspondence.

Jasper, Bernard. USS *Langley*. Interview.

Jones, David. USS *Langley*. Interview, private papers, and photos.

Kennedy, John. USS *Langley*. Interview, correspondence, and private papers.

Koepsell, Chester. USS *Langley*. Interview, correspondence, and photos.

Laforest, Thomas. USS *Whipple*. Interview, private papers, and photos.

Kownacki, Walter. USS *Langley*. Interview.

Martin, Jay. USS *Langley*. Interview, correspondence, and private papers.

Mayfield, Harvey. USS *Langley*. Interview.

McElroy, I. W. 51st. Pursuit Squadron. Correspondence.

McKinney, Millard. USS *Langley*. Interview and private papers.

Mealley, James. USS *Langley*. Interview, private papers, and photos.

Mickey, John. USS *Langley*. Correspondence.

Mills, Reginald. USS *Langley*. Interview.

Moorehead, James. 17th Pursuit Squadron. Interview and photos.

Onberg, Carl. USS *Langley*. Interview.

Restorff, Henry. USS *Langley*. Interview.

Sanders, Homer L. 51st Fighter Group. Interview, correspondence, and diary.

Saulton, James. USS *Langley*. Interview.

Schirmer, Frank R., Class 40-A historian. Correspondence.

Schwartz, Max R. USS *Langley*. Correspondence.

Shanley, Richard. USS *Langley*. Interview.

Shepston, Raymond. USS *Langley*. Interview.

Sinner, Walter. USS *Langley*. Interview.

Snay, Charles A. USS *Langley*. Interview, correspondence, and private papers.

Snyder, Earl. USS *Langley*. Interview.

Snyder, Marvin. USS *Langley*. Interview.

Spence, Gordon. 51st Fighter Group. Interview and correspondence.

Squire, Grant R. USS *Langley*. Correspondence and photos.

St. Pierre, Paul. USS *Langley*. Correspondence.

Van Deurs, George. USS *Langley*. Correspondence.

Watson, Walter R. USS *Langley*. Correspondence.

Wetherbee, Frank. USS *Langley*.

Whan, Howard. USS *Langley*. Interview.

Wheeler, Dr. Gerald. Naval Historian. Interview.

Documents

Abernethy, E. Paul. "Action and Sinking of USS *Pecos*, 1 March 1942." Naval Historical Center, Washington, D.C.

Binford, Thomas H. "Narrative," 11 April 1942. Naval Historical Center, Washington, D.C.

Blackwell, Dr. Robert. "USS *Langley*." Typewritten report, undated. The Covered Wagon Association, Newport News, VA, (a copy in the author's possession).

"Combat Narratives: The Java Sea Campaign" Copy No. 752, undated. The Naval Historical Center, Washington, D.C. (a copy in the author's possession).

Convoy and Routing Files., 10th Fleet, Convoy MS-5, Naval Historical Center, Washington, D.C.

Crouch, E. M. "Narrative," 4 April 1944. Naval Historical Center, Washington, D.C.

Glassford, William. "Narrative of Events in the South-West Pacific, 14 February–5 April 1942." Microfilm Nrs. 1970–71. Naval Historical Center, Washington, D.C.

"Interview with Lieutenant Gerald Dix," 10 December 1942. File 142:052DIX. Albert F. Simpson Historical Center, Maxwell AFB, AL.

"Kokan Senshi Nr. 26." (War History Nr. 26), undated. Japanese Aviation Historical Society, Hiroshima, Japan. Translated by Dr. George Moore, Ph.D., San Jose State University. (Copy and translation in the author's possession).

McConnell, Robert P. "Operations, Actions, and Sinking of USS *Langley*, 22 February–5 March 1942." 9 March 1942. Naval Historical Center, Washington, D.C.

Office of Naval Intelligence. "Attack on U.S. Naval Vessels by Japanese Airplanes," undated. Naval Historical Center, Washington, D.C.

Operations, Java Campaign File, Documents 707–960. Albert F. Simpson Historical Center, Maxwell AFB, AL.

"Report of Aircraft Accident, Akerman William P., 1st Lt., 2-28-43." Air Force Inspection and Safety Center Headquarters, Norton AFB, CA.

Rodgers Family Papers. The Library of Congress, Washington, D.C.

USS *Langley* (AV-3) Movement Card, 29 December 1941–27 February 1942. Naval Historical Center, Washington, D.C.

USS *Langley* Muster Rolls, 25 January 1939–10 March 1942. RG24, National Archives, General Archives Div., Washington, D.C.

USS *Langley*, Seaplane Tender." Visitor's brochure, May 1939, L. D. Chirillo, Todd Pacific Shipyards, Seattle, Washington. (Copy in the author's possession).

USS *Pecos* (AO-6) Movement Cards, 14 January 1941–5 May 1942. Naval Historical Center, Washington, D.C.

USS *Pecos*, Survivors' Narratives. Naval Personnel Command, Casualty Assistance Branch, Washington, D.C.

USS *Whipple* (DD-217) Deck Log, 26 February–6 March 1942. National Archives, Navy and Old Army Branch, Washington, D.C.

"Vice Admiral William A. Glassford, USN (deceased)," 1 August 1958. Naval Historical Center, Washington, D.C.

Books

Buell, Thomas B. *Master of Sea Power: A Biography of Fleet Admiral Ernest J. King*. Boston and Toronto: Little, Brown & Co. 1980.

Chief of Naval Operations, Naval History Division, *United States Naval Aviation, 1910–1970*. Washington, D.C.: GPO, 1970.

Cline, Joe C. "First Naval Aviation Unit in France." *Naval Aviation in World War I*, pp. 10–15. Edited by Adrian O. Van Wyen and the editors of *Naval Aviation News*. Washington, D.C.: GPO, 1969.

Craven, Wesley F., and Cate, James L., eds. *The Army Air Forces in World War II*, vol. 1: *Plans and Early Operations, January 1939 to August 1942*. Chicago: University Of Chicago Press, undated.

Edmonds, Walter D. *They Fought With What They Had: The Story of the Army Air Forces in the Southwest Pacific, 1941–1942*. Boston: Little, Brown & Co., 1951.

Francillon, Rene J. *Japanese Navy Bombers of World War II*. New York: Doubleday, 1969.

King, Ernest, and Whithill, Walter. *Fleet Admiral King: A Naval Record*. New York: Norton, 1952.

Liddell-Hart, B. H. *History of the Second World War.* New York: G. P. Putnam's Sons, 1970.

Melhorn, Charles M. *Two Block Fox: The Rise of the Aircraft Carrier, 1911–1929.* Annapolis: Naval Institute Press, 1974.

Morison, Sameul E. *History of United States Naval Operations in World War II*, vol. 3, *The Rising Sun in the Pacific, 1931–April 1942.* Boston: Little, Brown & Co., 1948.

Navy Department. *Dictionary of American Naval Fighting Ships*, vol. 2. Washington, D.C.: GPO, 1963.

Navy Department. *Dictionary of American Naval Fighting Ships*, vol. 4. Washington, D.C.: GPO, 1969.

Navy Department. *Dictionary of American Naval Fighting Ships*, vol. 5. Washington, D.C.: GPO, 1970.

Okumiya, Masatake, Horikoshi, Jiro and Cadin, Martin. *Zero.* New York: Ballantine, 1956.

Parkes, Oscar, and McMurtrie, Francis E., eds. *Jane's Fighting Ships, 1924.* London: Sampson Low Marston, 1924; reprint ed. New York: Arco Pub. Co., 1980.

Polmar, Norman. *Aircraft Carriers: A Graphic History of Carrier Aviation and Its Influence on World Events.* New York: Doubleday, 1969.

Van Oosten, F. C. *The Battle of the Java Sea.* The Sea Battles in Close-up Series. Annapolis: Naval Institute Press, 1976.

Wagner, Ray. *American Combat Airplanes.* New York: Doubleday, 1968.

Periodicals

Abernethy, E. Paul. "The *Pecos* Died Hard." U.S. Naval Institute *Proceedings*, December 1969, pp. 74–82.

Divoll, Lawrence E. *"Langley*'s Last Voyage." *Shipmate*, January–February 1981, pp. 19–20.

Editor. "The Death of USS *Edsall*: A Gallant Fight Against Impossible Odds." *Shipmate*, April 1980, p. 12.

Emmanuel, Michel G. "The Java Crapshoot." *Shipmate*, June 1972, pp. 19–24.

Grosvenor, Melville B. "The New Queen of the Sea." *The National Geographic*, vol. 82, July 1942, pp. 22–30.

Harrington, Skip H. "The Mystery of USS *Edsall*." *Shipmate*, January–February 1980, pp. 26–28.

Schwarz, Max R. "Service in USS *Langley* (CV-1) 1930–31." *The Hook*, fall 1979, pp. 6–9.

Souberman, Eugene. "Philippine Air Diary." *A.A.H.S. Journal*, winter 1968, pp. 240–56.

Tate, Jackson R. "We Rode the Covered Wagon." U.S. Naval Institute *Proceedings*, October 1978, pp. 62–69.

Van Deurs, George. "The First Carrier Plane Scouting Mission." U.S. Naval Institute *Proceedings*, October 1978, pp. 70–71.

Van Deurs, George. "Last Cruise of the *Langley*." *VFW Magazine*, April 1962, pp. 14–32.

Yon, J. L. "Doctor's at Sea." *Colliers*, 28 August 1943, pp. 12–21

Newspapers

New York Times, 16 April 1923 and 5 April 1942.

San Francisco Chronicle, 4 April 1942.

Index